BRIEF INTRODUCT

CW00497614

A concise law review on development
and use of technology

Asril Sitompul Agussalim

Christchurch – 2021

Asril Sitompul Agussalim: Brief introduction to Techlaw

*A concise law review on development
and use of technology*

ISBN: 9798526543170

Publisher:

BooksTerrace & Library

(Information Center for Indonesian Law)

Bandung, 2021

CONTENTS

Foreword

Development of information technology bring about significant changes to almost all aspects of everyday human life. The easier use of the Internet and broader access to broadband network connection support the wider of information technology-based services. Many kinds of services that formerly separated and provided by different providers, with the availability of broadband Internet based services have already converged.

In the field of law, information technology has changed the substances of law and law enforcement procedures. The changes forced all stakeholders in the field of law, economy, and business, especially they who involved in activities that related to information technology to pay attention and to have sufficient knowledge about law related to information technology.

This book purposes to discuss the legal issues happened in the recent development of technology. However, considering the broad of scope of technology development, this book to be limited to briefly discuss development of information, communication, and financial technology, Internet, Artificial Intelligence (AI), and matters related to technological developments commonly referred to as digital technology.

This book is not intended for technicians and people who work in technology every day, but for people who want to know about technology related to law and its problems. The discussion related to technology in this book is only an introduction so as not to be completely wonder about technology and its daily use.

In the preparation of this book, I received a lot of input and suggestions from friends, some are technology experts, there are also law scholars whose names cannot be mentioned one by one, for that I express my deep gratitude.

I hope this book will be useful for the readers.

Christchurch, New Zealand, 2021

The Author

I

INTRODUCTION

Science and Technology in Human Life

History has already revealed to us the importance of technology in human life. Since ancient time, people have struggled to improve their quality of life using a very basic and simple technology in line with their time. Since long time ago people needed technology in accordance with the development of time, from the making of equipment necessary to find the sources of food as axes of stone, then iron, the invention of gunpowder, to the make of weapons for hunting, the creation of devices to defend themselves from natural attacks, wild animals, and their fellow human enemies, or to attack other humans in order to maintain the continuity of food supplies and expand hunting, livestock or agricultural areas.

Nevertheless, the development of technology is a necessity that cannot be stopped. Since the beginning, technology has already become important means of supporting human life. However, it should be noted that from the outset, technology was not only used to support and provide convenience in human life, but it could also and tend to be used for purposes that could damage the order of human life, such as the use of technology for warfare, both as weapons and non-weapons equipment. It is an undeniable fact that almost all [new] technology is directly or indirectly used as weapons and used as a tool of war even though at first the inventor/creator of a new technology did not intend to use it as a tool for war.

Albert Einstein certainly did not intend to deliberately create his theory of relativity to create the atomic bombs which were then dropped on Hiroshima and Nagasaki which claimed millions of human lives. The Wright Brothers (Orville Wright and Wilbur Wright) who created airplanes also did not intend to make their creations to become bombers. Even though, there are also technological devices that are created and intended as tools of war, such as the creation of drone, so it is not surprising that drones are used to fly bombs and drop them into an area as a target. In general, technology was created to make it easier for humans to live their lives, but technological advances that are so fast and have a big impact on life of human being that make it difficult to curb and to control the use of technology. Technology in the fields of informatics, telecommunications, and computers was created to facilitate human life, but at the same time, crime is also developing in its use, for example, the types of *cyber-crime,* that uses various information technology, including *spam, cyber-bullying, deep-fake,* and other crimes rapidly growing as well. The tendency to use technology as a tool for self-defense or committing crimes has been a reality since the beginning of human civilization.

Cybercrime has attracted the attention of many parties, including the International Telecommunication Union stated that cybercrime and cybersecurity are issues that cannot be separated from an already interconnected environment and the UN General Assembly passed a resolution on cybersecurity in 2010, stated that cybercrime is one of the biggest challenges that must be faced.[1]

---

[1] International Telecommunication Union. *Understanding cybercrime: Phenomena, challenges, and legal response.* September 2012, p. 2.

Humans realize that efforts need to be made to prevent and limit the use of technology for purposes that have a negative impact on human life. But today we are faced with technological developments that are completely different and unknown in the past and of course the old laws and regulations are no longer appropriate and unable to regulate them. The change made some laws obsolete while the provisions of the new law did not yet exist.

With the development of technology and the use of Big Data, arise idea about the possibility of using algorithmic regulation, i.e., regulatory governance system that utilizes algorithmic decision making. Although the scope and meaning of 'regulation' and 'regulatory governance' in this matter is still debatable, some scholars define regulation or regulatory governance as an attempt to manage risk or change behavior to reach some preordained objectives.[2]

---

[2] Yeung, K. (2017) 'Algorithmic regulation: a critical interrogation', *Regulation & Governance*, doi: 10.1111/rego. 12158, in Martin Lodge, et.al. DISCUSSION PAPER No: 85, September 2017. London School of Economic and Political Sciences.

However, it should be noted that the wider social impact of people's increasing reliance on algorithms in everyday life has attracted considerable interest in recent years, especially with the increasing awareness of the power of Big Data and predictive analytics. One of the clearest examples is the widespread concern about the use of algorithms to manipulate information and therefore affect political life, especially at election time, for example the allegations of electoral fraud in the United States recently.

In the field of finance, the role of cryptocurrency is seen as an important development, where cryptographic algorithms play a crucial function, such as the use of algorithms to facilitate supply and demand for services around the world which called the 'gig economy'.[3] In this case, the attention of law makers and enforcers is urgently needed in order not to let the development take place without clear rules and regulations.

---

[3] Alex J Wood, et. al (2019). Good Gig, Bad Gig: Autonomy and Algorithmic Control in the Global Gig Economy. Work, Employment and Society 2019, Vol. 33(1) 56–75.

One of the technologies that development is very prominent today is computing technology, this is marked by very rapid progress in all aspects, namely speed, and increasing data storage capabilities, and last but not least is that the progress today has overcome the obstacles that existed in the past in terms of speed and data storage capabilities.

The development also overcome obstacles in terms of the price of storage facilities. For example, when compared with computers in the past, the IBM computer type 305 RAMC which at that time was the computer with the largest storage capacity (with a 5 Mb hard drive) the size was twice the size of a refrigerator today, and the price was around $ 10,000 per megabyte. Today a 500 Gigabyte hard drive is only the size of a human palm and costs less than a hundred dollars (that is less than 2 cents per megabyte).[4]

---

[4] Henri Arslanian and Fabrice Fischer (2019). *The Future of Finance. The Impact of FinTech, AI, and Crypto on Financial Services*. (Cham: Palgrave Macmillan), p. 6.

Category of Technology

Because it is really needed, humans are constantly developing technology in all fields. From the beginning and in its development, technology can be divided into three categories based on its use: first, technology to defend (defensive technology), the second is technology to attack (offensive technology) and the third, neutral technology. Defensive technology is technology developed by humans with the aim of defending themselves and maintaining life and the quality of human life. This technology was developed starting from how to make fire, sharpen spears, make bows and arrows, make traps for dangerous wild animals and to build fishing boats. Techniques for planting seeds ranging from rice, wheat, vegetables, agricultural tools to refining and seeding technology as well as crossing and refining food plant varieties. And if it continues to this day, it appears that there are technological developments in food canning and hydroponic plant cultivation and livestock grazing.

This defensive technology is intended to provide or improve the comfort of human life, as a continuation of the fulfillment of the basic needs of life. In this category, there is also the technology of making cars, airplanes, ships, trains, construction technology of skyscrapers and so on, will continue to develop without ending.

Offensive technology is a technology developed by humans to improve the comfort of life. However, with the encouragement of reduced hunting areas and the narrowing of agricultural land due to an increase in the number of group members or due to a decrease in the number of animals, there is a need to expand the area of agriculture or hunting, and in its use the developed technology goes hand in hand with the need to expand hunting areas and increase the area of agricultural land in addition to maintaining self-security and defending the group.

This expansion of agricultural land and hunting areas led to contact with other groups who also had the same needs. Instead of cooperating or merging their groups, most people chose to fight each other in the area, and these disputes required not only means of self-defense but also means of attacking other groups they consider as enemies. Starting from this expansion intention, the need arises for the development of offensive technologies, ranging from the creation of bows and arrows, weapons, cannons, to provide, if we proceed, the manufacture of nuclear bombs and chemical weapons.

Neutral technology. Now people have also thought about the existence of equipment and devices with technology known as technical neutrality devices, which can be used and developed for all purposes, defending, attacking, or improving the quality of human life, such as technologies related to robotics, artificial intelligence (AI), intelligent machines (machine learning), or the development of the highest level of intelligence, namely superintelligence. But the truth about the neutrality of technology is still questionable because it will go back to the humans who develop and use it. Human nature, which always looking for ways to satisfy their desires is the biggest obstacle in maintaining the neutrality of technology.

However, from a legal point of view, the three categories of technology, if used properly by the right parties, will greatly assist in the formation, application, and development of law. Conversely, if used incorrectly by the wrong party, it can also lead to the destruction of the law, although it must be admitted that the law will not match or precede technological developments.

Technology is proven as a powerful tool for preventing law violations. Starting from traffic violations to more serious and more sophisticated crimes such as crimes via the internet, banking fraud, money laundering, and other frauds can also be prevented with technology. Various systems that are useful in people's lives can be improved by using technology. Tax payment systems, voter registration systems for general elections, and even electoral systems can also be made with technology, and with the use of appropriate technology will be able to prevent or at least reduce the possibility of violations.

Traffic control using technology has been commonly used in developed and developing countries. The presence of traffic cameras that monitor vehicle speed, and monitor traffic density, if used properly and actively, will be able to prevent or at least reduce traffic violations. Security in buildings and vital infrastructure using high-level technology will be more powerful to prevent disturbances than deploying security guards.

Prevention of pollution of rivers, lakes and the environment can be done by using technology, which is applied to sources of pollution such as factories and other industries, as well as applied to protection systems in places that are prone to possible contamination.

The development of technology and its use in various fields raises the need for new regulations. Many laws and regulations have been around for a long time, but the emergence of additional requirements every year, due to the complexity of growth and the data requirements used by various parties put regulations at risk of falling behind. For example, laws related to anti-money laundering (AML) and fraud prevention require advanced analytical techniques to be able to adapt to technological growth.

In its development, technology requires legal regulations that can be used to guard its use in various fields of life. The EU data protection law is an example of limitation of the use of technology in making decision. The EU data protection law gives a person the right not to be the subject of a fully automated decision based on his profile and equips him with the right to know the logical reasons for the decision.[5]

Law and Technology

Along with the development of technology, as examples above, legal scholars and practitioners do not mislaid trying to follow it by developing legal regulations relating to the creation and use of technology in various fields with the aim of formulating legal regulations and provisions that can prevent the impact of the use of bad technology and as far as possible to be able to impose the necessary sanctions in the event of a violation in the creation and use of a new technology.

An understanding of the nature of the relationship between law and technology is essential to understand how modern society and government run. The relationship between law and technology is reciprocal, namely: law regulates technology, both by prohibiting

---

[5] Lee A. Bygrave (2017). EU Data Protection Law Falls Short as Desirable Model for Algorithmic Regulation. In Martin Lodge, *et.al*. DISCUSSION PAPER No: 85, September 2017. London School of Economic and Political Sciences. See also: Data Protection Directive (95/46/EC), Article 15.

and regulating certain forms of technology, and by encouraging or protecting other forms, on the other hand technology is also an important supporter for the effectiveness of the law.

Nevertheless, at this time, it must be recognized that the role of technology in preventing crime is very significant, with a good technology architecture, the possibility of crime will be prevented or at least minimized. For example, a system made with the right technology will be more effective in preventing bribery of officials related to the receipt of tax payments, because taxpayers do not have to deal with officers or officials if payments can be made through banks, ATMs or through internet banking.

II

THE INTERNET

Development of the Internet

Since the development of the idea of a system of connectivity that connects several computer terminals at MIT in 1962,[6] which then continued to grow until in the 1990s, the Internet had surpassed its initial research objectives and gave birth to the first *world wide web* (www) link system and browser in 1993.[7]

The Internet is an international network that communicates using TCP/IP (*Transmission Control Protocol/ Internet Protocol*) programs, which is the basis of the Internet communication protocol. In the 1970s the TCP/IP model was created by the Defense Advanced

---

[6] For the development of the Internet, see: Robert Kahn, *et. al.* (1997). The Evolution of the Internet as a Global Information System. *The International Information & Library Review, 29:2, 129-151.*

[7] Sally J. Mcmillan & Margaret Morrison (2006). Coming of age with the internet: A qualitative exploration of how the internet has become an integral part of young people's lives. *New Media & Society 8(1):73–95.*

Research Projects Agency (DARPA), a research division of the United States Department of Defense (DOD), for use on the ARPANET, a wide area network (WAN). which was the forerunner of the Internet.[8]

TCP/IP is a program that consists of two levels. The high level is the Transmission Control Protocol (TCP), and the low level is the Internet Protocol (IP). TCP divides a message or a file into small packets which are then sent over the Internet and received at the destination by TCP which rearranges according to the original message or file and IP handles the address and delivery route to ensure that the packet or file arrives at the right destination.[9]

TCP/IP was originally designed for UnixOS and has been built into all operating systems (Operating System – OS) created since. Now the TCP/IP model and associated protocols are managed by the Internet Engineering Task Force (IETF).[10]

The development of the Internet is indeed very fast, when viewed from its original creation, the use of the

---

[8] Michael L. Rustad (2016). *Global Internet Law in A Nutshell®*. *Third Edition*. St Paul Minn: West Academic Publishing.
[9] Margaret Rouse (2015). *TCP/IP*. Techtarget.com.
[10] *Ibid.*

Internet was passive, where forums and bulletin boards were the exclusive way to post information, this stage is called Web 1.0. At the stage of Web 1.0 the Internet offered little interactivity. Then the Internet entered the era of Web 2.0. At Web 2.0 users are connected through blogs and social media. The *www* exists on Web 2.0 and is still in the process of developing into Web 3.0. Web 3.0 is also continuing to develop but is not predicted to replace Web 2.0 completely. Web 3.0 is evolving into the Internet of Things (IoT) where smart devices communicate from humans to computers and from computers to computers.[11] However, nowadays people rarely use the terms Web 1.0, Web 2.0, or Web 3.0.

As a relatively new innovation that develops very quickly (when compared to other systems such as telephone, radio and television),[12] now the Internet has

---

[11] Michael L. Rustad (2016). *Op cit.*, p. 21.

[12] P. K. Downes (2007). An introduction to the Internet. *British Dental Journal Volume 202 No. 5 - Mar 10, 2007*: *"It is evident from the fact that it took radio 38 years to reach 50 million listeners in America. Television reached 50 million viewers within 14 years. While the Internet reached 50 million users in just 4 years."* See also: S. Srinivasan (2014). Cloud Computing Basics. New York: Springer: *"Technology device lifespan*

become a basic ingredient in personal and professional life. With the increasing use of the internet people are introduced to new innovations based on internet technology making life easier socially, politically, and economically. Internet is also changing the way people consume news, transact business, communicate, socialize, the way people enjoy leisure time with entertainment, and even the way they shop for groceries.[13]

Many people have high expectation in the development of the Internet. Some argue that the internet can drive transformation of individuals, societies, cultures and organizations. The internet has given birth to a form of community called a networked society or referred to as a networked citizen (netizen) which is a transformation of social, technological, economic and cultural integration.

Some people hope that the internet can be used as a tool to defeat totalitarianism and tyranny, although there

reaches 50 million users: Phone 75 years; Radio 38 years; Television 13 years; Personal Computer 16 years; Internet 4 years; Google Search Engine 3 months; YouTube 11 months; Facebook 2 years 10 months and Twitter 3 years."

[13] Jonathan B. Brown (2020). Casting a Broad Net: The Federal Communication Commission's Preemption of State Broadband Internet Regulation. *Creighton Law Review [Vol. 54. 2020].*

are also those who worry that the internet becomes a tool for criminals and the spread of rumors and slander. Furthermore, the internet is also said to be a driver that leads to eradication of poverty, economic development, government communication media, and as resources and tools to improve business processes.[14]

In addition, the Internet revolution is driving human-to-human connectivity on an unprecedented scale. The revolution that will occur next is predicted to be interconnection between objects to create a 'smart environment'. In 2011, the number of interconnected

---

[14] Kallol K. Bagchi, *et. al.* (2015). Internet use and human values: Analyses of developing and developed countries. *Computers in Human Behavior 50 (2015) 76–90.* See also: Alcántara-Pilar, *et. al.* (2013). A cross-cultural analysis of the effect of language on perceived risk online. *Computers in Human Behavior, 29(3), 596–603*; Bagchi, K., Hart, P., & Peterson, M. (2004). IT product adoption and the influence of national culture. *Journal of Global Information Technology Management, 7(4), 29–46*; Castells, Manuel (1998, second edition, 2000). End of Millennium, The Information Age: Economy, Society and Culture, Vol. III. Cambridge, MA; Oxford, UK: Blackwell; Zhang, X., Pablos, P. O., & Xu, Q. (2014). Culture effects on the knowledge sharing in multi-national virtual classes: A mixed method. *Computers in Human Behavior, 31, 491–498*; and Leiner, B. V., *et al.* (1999). A brief history of the Internet. *Communications of the ACM, 40(2), 102–108.*

devices in the world exceeded the number of people on earth. From the recently around 9 billion connected devices, that number surpassed 20.4 billion in 2020,[15] the number is greater than the predictions of the GSM Association (GSMA). In April 2021, the GSMA estimates that there are 8.8 billion cellular connections in the world including IoT connections, while cellular phone subscribers account for 5.1 billion.[16]

In overcoming challenges and obstacles which at the same time become opportunities, operators are trying to provide new services and bundling their products to provide value-added services to retain their customers. The development of cellular and Internet services, provided by OTT or conventional providers to promote IoT, requires the provision of a wide bandwidth frequency spectrum, by wireless network or by fiber optic network to the home (FTTH).

---

[15] Noura Alhakbani, *et. al.* An efficient event matching system for semantic smart data on the Internet of Things (IoT) environment. *Future Generation Computer Systems 95 (2019) 163–174.*

[16] GSMA Global Data April 2021.

Based on forecasts from various parties Machine-to-Machine (M2M) interconnection will be able to peak in 2021, generating huge market opportunities, especially in the machine-to-machine (M2M) and consumer electronics sectors. According to GSMA (2018), there will be a revenue opportunity of USD 1.3 trillion for mobile communication network operators including their vertical segments such as healthcare, automotive, public services, and electronics houseware.[17]

Supported by the development of the Internet of Things (IoT), also equipped with an increase in companies using cloud services and with the support of developing equipment using wireless technology such as bluetooth, radio frequency identification (RFID), Wi-Fi, and telephone data services and coupled with more sophisticated sensor capabilities, IoT has undergone a transformation and transformed the use of the Static Internet into a Fully Integrated Future Internet.[18]

---

[17] GSMA: 2018 State of the Industry Report on Mobile Money.
[18] Giuseppe Rugger (2020). The Internet of Things for Smart Environments. *Future Internet 2020, 12, 51.*

The question in this case, is whether such a sophisticated progress can be regulated by existing legal instruments, or whether a new legal instrument is needed that can adopt all the progress that has occurred. Experts at ITU already predict the legal problems that will arise related to IoT. From the ICT policy maker and regulator point of view some of the challenges in legal aspect, will be among others: Licensing, spectrum allocation, standard operability, tariffs, and data protection. [19]

Internet Utilization

Internet has proven useful in human life. By using internet technology, tax payment systems, voter registration systems for general elections, and even general election systems have also become easier and can also prevent or at least reduce the possibility of violations.[20] Likewise, with the use of internet technology, revealing of criminal cases and criminal acts

---

[19] ITU Academy. https://www.itu.int/en/ITU-D/Regional-Pre sence/AsiaPacific/Documents/Events/2018/IoT-BDG.

[20] Asril Sitompul (2014). *Menggugat Moral Bangsa. Studi Tentang Hukum dan Moralitas*. (Bandung: BooksTerrace & Library), p. 143.

will be done faster and more accurately. In this case it appears that technology is very helpful in the legal field in preventing or reducing law violations.

However, the development of the Internet has not gone unnoticed by criminals, who view that technology can be used as a tool to commit crimes and violate the law. In line with the development of the internet, crimes that use the internet are also growing, ranging from bank break-in, money laundering, and fraud that occurs using the internet.

This has happened since the beginning of the development of the Internet. For example, the famous 1994 internet bank robbery case was carried out by Vladimir Levin from his apartment in St. Petersburg, Russia. Levin, a computer programmer, is accused of hacking the accounts of several customers of large corporate Citibank and earning $10.7 million. In collaboration with his colleagues around the world, Levin transferred large amounts of cash to banks accounts in

Finland, the United States, the Netherlands, Germany, and Israel.[21]

Now, crimes on the Internet or those committed using the Internet are becoming easier to be committed and thus are occurring more frequently and without boundaries. In 2020, the National Cybersecurity Operations Center (Pusopskamsinas) of the National Cyber and Crypto Agency (BSSN) in Indonesia, noted that 88,414,296 cyberattacks had occurred from January 1 to April 12, 2020. In January there were 25,224,811 cybercrimes and in February 29,188,645 cases, then in March there were 26,423,989 cases and up to April 12, 2020, there were 7,576,851 cases had been recorded.[22]

The peak number of cyberattack cases occurred on March 12, 2020, which reached 3,344,470 cases and then experienced a significant decline when the work from home (WFH) policy was implemented in various places in Indonesia. During WFH there have been cyberattacks

---

[21] Marc Goodman (2015). *Future crimes: everything is connected, everyone is vulnerable and what we can do about it.* (New York, Toronto: Doubleday), p. 20.
[22] https://bssn.go.id/rekap-serangan-siber-januari-april-2020/ Accessed January 27, 2021.

that take advantage of issues related to Covid-19. The most common type is trojan activity, which is 56% and then followed by information gathering activity as much as 43% of the total cyberattacks, while the remaining 1% are web application attacks.[23]

Data compiled by BSSN, as of April 12, 2020, there have been 25 cybercrimes using the background of the Covid-19 pandemic issue, of which there are 17 cases targeted globally and 8 cases targeting countries. In January and February each occurred one cybercrime using the background of the Covid-19 pandemic, the case was Malicious Email Phishing. In March there were the most cases, reaching 22 cybercrimes using the background of the Covid-19 pandemic issue, these cases occurred with various types including Trojan HawkEye Reborn, Blackwater malware, Hidden Ad (Android), Metasploit, Xerxes Bot, and Covid19 Tracker Apps.[24]

In April 2020 there was only one cybercrime that used the background of the Covid-19 pandemic issue, the case was Malicious Zoom. On April 1, 2020, a cyber case was

---

[23] *Op cit.*
[24] *Op cit.*

recorded using the background of the Covid-19 pandemic issue on the Zoom application globally, where this application was inserted by Malicious Zoom which uses coding containing metasploit modules, adware and hiddenad/ hiddad.[25]

In the field of crime prevention and control, the Internet has also been proven to play a role through facial recognition applications through surveillance cameras that are connected to Big Data. In China the network of surveillance cameras installed has exceeded the number of 170 million units. By using facial recognition technology, the police have been able to arrest economic crime suspects who were watching a pop star concert in Nanchang city. With the help of the facial recognition program, the police could easily and quickly identify and arrest suspects who were among the more than 60,000 people who attended the concert.[26]

However, the use of facial recognition in China is opposed by various parties, including one who has filed a

---

[25] https://bssn.go.id. *Op cit.*
[26] BBC News April 13, 2018. *Chinese man caught by facial recognition at pop concert. https://www.bbc.com/news/world-asia-china-43751276.* Accessed April 19, 2021.

lawsuit in court. The Fuyang District People's Court in East Zhejiang province ruled that the amusement park's Hangzhou Safari Park using facial recognition technology without visitors' consent to facilitate entry to the park was 'unauthorized and unnecessary'. The court ruling was handed down on a lawsuit by Guo Bing (a law professor from Zhejiang Sci-Tech University) and his wife who sued the amusement park on charges of violating consumer protection laws by taking sensitive personal information without their consent.[27]

The monitoring system with facial recognition is being challenged by various parties, because there are those who argue that the monitoring system violates the community's right of freedom of movement and activity without being followed by a monitoring system. The monitoring system should not turn a country into an 'Orwellian state' as stated by George Orwell in his book "1984."

---

[27] Gigi Onag (2020). Court ruled on China's first case over facial recognition tech. Future IoT November 26, 2020. https://futureiot.tech/court-ruled-on-chinas-first-case-over-facial-recognition-tech. Accessed April 19, 2021.

The Matters of Internet Regulatory

From the previous discussion, it appears that the various services that were once separate can no longer be separated and must also be discussed together, because technologically services such as radio, television, telephone and internet can already be provided on the same network. In compiling regulations, regulators need to pay attention to this matter, both in drafting technical regulations and in formulating business regulations, because with this convergence, regulations that were previously relatively uncoordinated, must be thoroughly reconsidered so that they can work together and not contradict or overlap each other.

The reason why radio, television, cable, satellite, wireline telephone, cellular telephone and internet should be discussed in an integrated discussion, is because the market for these services has converged, but one thing that should be a major concern for regulators is the possibility that business competition cannot run because of the possibility of monopolies by large operators, and also that this is not desired by small operators, so there is a possibility of obstacles from operators who are still running their business separately.

Pros and cons of regulation

There is an opinion that says that the Internet needs to be regulated, because without regulation the rights of users in cyberspace will be ignored and the real-world laws will also be violated. Cyberspace, if not regulated would has the potential to endanger the legal system, may hinder activities in cyberspace itself, and at the end can reduce community values.[28] However, there are also opinions that oppose the regulation of the Internet, one of which is a group called Digital Libertarianism. According to this group, the law will not be able to apply effectively in cyberspace and therefore regulation must emphasize social norms and the concept of self-regulation.[29]

From the pros and cons regarding Internet regulation, the following will discuss about Internet regulations that exist in several countries although in practice there are

---

[28] Yee Fen LIM (2003). Law and Regulation in cyberspace. *Proceedings of the 2003 International Conference on Cyberworlds (CW'03) 0-7695-1922-9/03.*
[29] Jonathan B. Brown (2020). *Op cit.*

difficulties in regulating the Internet in total, because in accordance with its global nature and form, the types of actions taken, or events that occur on the Internet. or those who use the Internet are also global in nature. For example, Cyberwarfare, according to its form is a global phenomenon, like cyberterrorism. And because there are no international treaties governing data privacy, businesses often have no other way than to follow national government law and regulations that require compliance as a condition for doing business in certain country.

The form and nature of Internet regulation

The Internet is international network: therefore, most Internet problems require addressing globally or transnationally. However, not all problems that occur on the Internet are international issues, some problems are local issues. Cyberspace poses unavoidable jurisdictional problems because the Internet involves cross-border communication in almost all countries in the world. For example, the use of cloud services brings new challenges to law enforcement. Cloud computing, which is Internet-based computing, provides information and data services over the Internet, without the need for specific hardware or software at a physical access point, and can be accessed from different countries and jurisdictions.[30]

The issue of extraterritoriality gives rise to a new dimension as in cloud computing because the physical location of hardware and the location of data cross country boundaries and may not be known to users, thereby raising questions about the jurisdiction of each country crossed. Processing on cloud computing can occur in several countries at the same time. In a situation like this there is more than one country that both have jurisdiction over crimes committed through cloud computing, according to one of the jurisdictional bases that apply to the problem at hand.[31]

Although no single country can claim sovereignty over cyberspace, every country can exercise its sovereign prerogative over cyber infrastructure in its territory also

---

[30] Nancy J. King and V.T. Raja (2013). What Do They Really Know About Me in the Cloud? A Comparative Law Perspective on Protecting Privacy and Security of Sensitive Consumer Data. *Am. Bus. L.J.* 50.
[31] *Op cit.*

over activities related to the cyber infrastructure.[32] This prerogative includes jurisdiction, which is the authority of the state to regulate the activities of a person or legal entity with its national law.[33]

Even though it is recognized that cyberlaw transcends national boundaries, there are no conventions, laws, or guidelines that can cover all issues that occur on the Internet, such as computer security issues, electronic contracts, cybertorts, cybercrimes, online privacy, intellectual property, content cross-border jurisdictional rules or regulations.[34]

To deal with Internet issues of an international nature, the UN Secretariat has formed a working group that deals with Internet governance, namely the Working Group on Internet Governance (WGIG) which aims to provide input for the information community at the World Summit on the Information Society (WSIS). Transnational Internet

---

[32] Michael N. Schmitt. Ed. (2013), *Tallinn Manual on the International Law Applicable to Cyber Warfare* (Cambridge: Cambridge University Press), p. 15-16.

[33] Kriangsak Kittichaisaree (2017). *Public International Law of Cyberspace*. (Switzerland: Springer International Publishing), p. 24.

[34] Michael L. Rustad (2016). *Op cit.*, p. 45.

Governance or Transnational Internet Governance is needed as an alternative to hinder the control of top-down rulemaking by one country that has power.

In dealing with international and transnational issues, WGIG proposed the establishment of a Global Internet Council (GIC) consisting of representatives from governments of various countries. This GIC was designed to replace the Internet Corporation for Assigned Names and Numbers (ICANN). The plan is that GIC will replace ICANN and make policies more transparent and with greater public participation due to the role of the UN. The goal is that the GIC will synchronize public policy in cyberspace and oversee the management of Internet resources.

For example, GIC will supervise IP addresses, introduce new top-level domains (TLDs), and assign country code top-level domains (ccTLDs). Examples of ccTLDs are: .us (for United States) and .de (for Germany). Another draft of the WGIG is the establishment of the International Internet Council (IIC) which will replace ICANN's Government Advisory Committee (GAC). IIC will spearhead public policies such as Internet resource management and universal access. The IIC will resolve Internet resource management issues and institutionalize transparent and democratic decision-making in a coordinated manner. Eurozone governance, for example, emphasizes the need for open, transparent, and orderly dialogue between the European Union and various other sectors of civil society.

On the other hand, there are those who predict the end of the global nature of the Internet due to rumors that China in the future will establish a separate root system for their Internet share. As the roots split, the United States and its allies must form a coalition of democratic states that will offer a firm choice and a clear alternative to China's model of Internet governance around the world. At the same time, the Chinese government with the support of Russia and other totalitarian regimes will set up a separate root system on their Internet, and if this split occurs it will signal the end of the global Internet era.[35]

---

[35] Robert K. Knake (2019). The Beginning of the End of the Open Internet Era. *Council of Foreign Relation, January 6, 2020.*

For national level regulations, various countries have issued laws related to activities on the Internet, whether in the form of business transactions, trade, as well as activities in the form of violations of the law and criminal acts. Governments in several countries often carry out their will extraterritorially in cyberspace through regulations and guidelines (directives).

For example, the European Commission since decades ago (1995) has given European citizens the right to control the collection, transmission or use of personal information. The European Community's Data Protection Directive prohibits the transfer of personal information across national borders unless the receiving country has implemented an adequate level of protection.[36]

Subsequently, the General Data Protection Regulation (GDPR) was enacted on May 25, 2018. The GDPR is the most stringent personal data privacy and security law in the world. Although designed and authorized by the European Union, it imposes obligations

---

[36] Directive 95/46 on the protection of individuals with regard to the processing of personal data and on the free movement of such data [1995] OJ L281/31.

on organizations everywhere, if they target or collect data related to people in the European Union.[37] The European Union's Data Protection Regulation gave European residents a right called the 'right to be forgotten' except for the right to express an opinion.[38]

The legal problems that exist in the use of personal data, not only the need for protection against misuse of personal data but have also extended to the need to determine the period of data storage by the party who collects and stores a person's personal data. For example, how long can Facebook, WhatsApp, or Twitter keep a user's personal data after that person no longer uses the social media. The right to be deleted from this data is known as the 'right to be forgotten'. The case that is often taken as an example is the 'drunken pirate case'.[39]

---

[37] Lennin Hernández González (2013). Habeo Facebook ergo sum? Issues around privacy and the right to be forgotten and the freedom of expression on online social networks, *Ent. L.R. 2013, 24(3), 83-87.*

[38] Tatiana-Eleni Synodinou, et.al. Editors (2017). *EU Internet Law. Regulation and Enforcement.* (Cham, Switzerland: Springer), p.7.

[39] Stacey Snyder v. Millersville University, et al. December 3, 2008.

III

INFORMATION AND COMMUNICATION
TECHNOLOGY

Data Collection, Storage and Computing

Along with the progress of information and communication technology which is experiencing rapid development, as well as the increasing use of computer technology and internet networks; these technological advances have an impact on an increasingly globalized economy and industry. The infrastructure and services, and information and communication sectors are also experiencing the impact of the revolution with the convergence of technology, infrastructure, and types of services.

Generally, the use of information and communication systems has a broad and complex structure and there are also several obstacles be the limitation.[40] The

---

[40] Mitsuo Gena and Osamu Katai (2009). Evolutionary Computation Technology and its Application. *Transactions On*

development of the use of large amounts of data requires a computing system that is faster and more accurate; it appears that the various problems that occur today are difficult to solve by using conventional computing methods, which still have relatively slow computation velocity.

The importance of data storage technology is related to the increasing importance of the use and utilization of data for different exigencies, nowadays in various activities: economic, political, and other fields, the availability of data in large forms and quantities is increasingly required. The need for data in large forms and quantities must also be supported by the ability and capacity of large data storage and processing.

Therefore, experts are constantly researching and developing practical optimization methods that can be applied to complex problems that occur in today's real world. For this reason, several applied computing evolution studies have been carried out to optimize combinations of the use of various systems, including the

Electrical and Electronic Engineering. IEEJ Trans 2009; 4: 34–35.

use of information systems and communication networks, image and voice processing, pattern recognition, control systems, prediction systems, reliability and ease of service, intelligent interfaces, humanoid robots, and security circuits system as well as parallel distributed systems.[41]

From the results of this research and development, various developments have been obtained in systems for compiling, collecting, storing, and computing data, which have recently become a concern.

The legal problem that arises in this case is regarding the procedure for collecting data originating from personal data, which is often done without the real consent of the data owner. Data collected from social media sources, for example, only gets indirect approval from the approval of the terms and conditions proposed by providers without any choice. It can be said that people are forced to give a sign of agreement because there is no other choice.

---

[41] Mitsuo Gena and Osamu Katai (2009). *Op cit.*

Quantum Computing

Advances in computing technology have an important role in the development of various sectors including economics and finance, especially with the development of quantum computing. With the development of the economic and financial sectors, so does the use of big data and applications. People who have been frustrated with desktop computers that are very slow when running large applications that require large data such as opening high-resolution digital photos or running several applications simultaneously, are now greatly helped by the emergence of quantum computing systems.

In the past, people tried to increase speed (usually short term) by installing additional memory called Random Access Memory (RAM) which was of course expensive. Unlike on a hard drive, data stored in RAM can be retrieved quickly in any order, making it suitable for its role as a temporary storage medium for computer processing while running programs. Now people are trying to overcome process lags by using quantum computers that take advantage of the quantum form of RAM in proper function.

Quantum computing is an attempt to present new computational capabilities by exploiting the complex nature of subatomic particles, and often contrary to what is commonly used around the world, through a branch of physics called quantum mechanics. These subatomic particles do not behave in the same way as physical objects in everyday activities, which have a clear position and positional characteristics, rather, subatomic particles exhibit a state called a 'super position' in which they can effectively be in many places at once.[42]

This state turned out to be important for computing. Quantum computers are the same as traditional computers, from the most basic calculators to the most powerful supercomputers, they all perform calculations using a 'binary code' where all data is encoded as a series of ones or zeros called bits, but through a 'super position', a bit quantum (quantum bit or qubit) can be in a state as one and zero together at the same time.[43] In a quantum

---

[42] See: G. P. Berman and G. D. Doolen. (2000). Solid-state quantum computation - a new direction for nanotechnology. *Superlattices and Microstructures, Vol. 27, No. 2/3, 2000.*

[43] Henri Arslanian and Fabrice Fischer (2019). *The Future of Finance. The Impact of FinTech, AI, and Crypto on Financial Services.* (Cham: Palgrave Macmillan), p. 4-5.

computer, information is stored in quantum bits or 'qubits', which can be thought of as pairs of quantum states that are part of the 'artificial atoms' created by quantum mechanics. There are various ways to create such artificial atoms, from ions, which are systems of atoms, to devices made of billions of atoms such as quantum dots, which under the right circumstances behave like atomic systems.[44]

Some processing can be done much faster in a quantum computer. Since a quantum computer is an improvement over a classical computer it will always be faster than a classical computer. But the high cost of processing qubits and the nature of most word-processing applications do not make much sense for using 'quantum' speeds.[45] So quantum processing is only beneficial if it is used for computations that require high speed.

Although quantum computing technology is a complex technology, however, the field of quantum

---

[44] James N. Eckstein and Jeremy Levy, Eds. (2013). Materials issues for quantum computation. *MRS BULLETIN VOLUME 38 OCTOBER 2013*.

[45] Emanuel Knill (2010). Quantum computing. NATURE | Vol 463 | 28 January 2010.

computing has now reached a stage where remote computing can be performed with minimal knowledge of hardware architecture. In addition, the relevant software to run on computers and quantum simulators is publicly available. Cloud access and cloud services to multiple quantum processors now allow the wider scientific community to explore the potential of quantum computing algorithms and devices.[46] Several studies report significant progress and show evidence of the benefits of using 'quantum RAM'.

In addition, people have also tried to apply hybrid quantum systems, which have been developed as a potential way to develop quantum computers. Recent research has shown that quantum hybrids provide the perfect solution for developing a form of RAM for quantum computers.

Cloud Computing

Cloud computing is a global technology that offers alternative information systems for all types of

---

[46] E. F. Dumitrescu. Cloud Quantum Computing of an Atomic Nucleus. Quant-ph, 11 January 2018.

businesses. The name cloud computing is inspired by the cloud symbol that is often used to represent the Internet in flow charts and diagrams.[47]

Cloud computing is a computing system that uses a technology known as virtualization, where one host computer runs an application called a hypervisor. This hypervisor application 'creates' one or more virtual machines (VM), which can simulate (imitate) computer devices precisely so that the simulation can run all software, from the operating system to end-user applications. The hypervisor, which is software capable of 'thinking', has access to the processor, network, and disk drives, all to itself just like on a 'real' (not virtual) computer.[48]

The hypervisor can perform all control functions, and can stop, delete, or 'create' a new virtual machine at any time. When coupled with extensive data center and

---

[47] Dimitrios Zissis and Dimitrios Lekkas (2012). Addressing cloud computing security issues. Future Generation Computer Systems 28 (2012) 583–592.
[48] Andrew R. Riddle and Soon M. Chung (2015). A Survey on the Security of Hypervisors in Cloud Computing. 2015 IEEE 35th International Conference on Distributed Computing Systems Workshops. *DOI 10.1109/ICDCSW.2015.28*.

management software, this technology enables cloud providers to achieve enormous economies of scale. And with-it users will also be able to access the cloud to compute as much as they want, and whenever they want.[49]

The term cloud computing invites different interpretations and views, some view that cloud computing is included in the field of computing engineering, while others consider that the cloud is a type of service, and some see it as a combination of technology, services, and activities. Some experts say that cloud computing is the provision of hardware, software systems, and applications delivered over the Internet.[50]

Over the last decade, cloud computing has received great attention from academia, industry, and government as a new infrastructure. This is because cloud computing requires less investment than using a hardware platform, also in terms of training costs, or the cost of paying for new software licenses. In addition, cloud services also

---

[49] Erica Naone (2009). Conjuring Clouds. How engineers are making on-demand computing a reality. *MIT Technology Review. June 23, 2009.*

[50] Nick Antonopoulos and Lee Gillam, Eds. (2010). *Cloud Computing. Principles, Systems and Applications*. (London: Springer).

promise savings for their users, because the cloud shifts the responsibility from the customer to install and maintain hardware and basic computing services remotely, for example from laboratories or consortia or corporate data centers to cloud vendors.[51]

Therefore, the cloud has also become very popular for businesses who need computing without having to have their own devices. In addition, flexible services allow users to adjust their usage capacity according to the needs of their business.

As a form of global network, the cloud is evolving rapidly, even in the absence of global standards. There is no common definition of cloud computing, different parties give different definitions. However, the National Institute of Standards and Technology (NIST) in America, although it does not provide a clear definition, NIST provides guidance on the nature and characteristics of cloud computing, namely that there are: five main

---

[51] Arnon Rosenthal, *et. al.* (2010). Cloud computing: A new business paradigm for biomedical information sharing. Journal of Biomedical Informatics 43 (2010) 342–353.

characteristics of cloud, four cloud distribution models, and three cloud service models.[52]

The five main characters of cloud are:[53] (i) Self Service. Services provided on request mean that consumers can request and receive access to service offerings, without an administrator or support staff to manually fulfill requests. The request process and fulfillment process are all automated. This offers advantages for both service providers and consumers; (ii) Wide Network Access. Cloud services must be easily accessible. Users are only required to have a basic network connection to connect to the service or application. In most cases, the connection used is some type of internet connection. Even though internet connections are growing in bandwidth, they are still relatively slow compared to local area network (LAN) connections. Because of this, the provider does not have to require users to have large amounts of bandwidth to use the service; (iii) Resource Pooling. Resource pooling

---

[52] Derrick Rountree (2014). *The basics of cloud computing: understanding the fundamentals of cloud computing in theory and practice*. (Waltham, MA: Elsevier), p. 2.
[53] Derrick Rountree (2014), *Op cit,* p. 3-5.

helps save costs and allows flexibility on the provider side. Resource pooling is because clients will not have a constant need for all the resources available to them. When a resource is not used by one customer, it can be used by another customer. This gives providers the ability to serve more customers than they could if each customer required a dedicated resource; (iv) Fast Elasticity. Rapid elasticity illustrates the ability of the cloud to grow easily to meet user demands. Cloud deployments must already have the required infrastructure in place to expand service capacity. If the system is designed properly, this may simply require adding more computer resources, hard disks, and the like. Their key is that even though resources are available, they are not used until they are needed. This allows providers to save on consumption costs (e.g., power and cooling); and (v) Scalable Service. Cloud services must have the ability to measure usage. Usage can be quantified using various metrics, such as time used, bandwidth used, and data used. The scalable characteristics of cloud computing services are those that enable the 'pay as you go' feature. Once the appropriate metrics have been identified, then the rate amount is determined. This rate is used to determine how much the customer should be charged. In this way, the customer is billed based on the level of consumption. If the service is not used on a certain day, the customer is not charged for that time.

Presently, there are 4 types of cloud computing, namely: public cloud, private cloud, hybrid cloud, and community cloud.

Public cloud or external cloud allows all users outside the site to use the resources available over the Internet through Web applications or Web services. Private cloud or internal cloud is created for the exclusive use of one user, who is personally responsible for its management and supervision. Hybrid cloud is a combination of several public cloud and private cloud platforms. Community cloud is a type of cloud hosting where it is possible to share among certain community organizations such as trading companies and banks.

All these cloud models are made to provide resources according to user demand accompanied by efforts to ensure quality of service and hardware/CPU performance, bandwidth, and memory capacity as well as an autonomous and transparent management system.

According to Sinivasan (2014), the types of cloud services defined by NIST consist of three basic services, namely infrastructure services (IaaS), platform services (PaaS), and software services (SaaS).[54]

Infrastructure as a Service (IaaS) provides the customer with the same features as PaaS, but the customer is fully responsible for controlling the infrastructure it leases. IaaS can be viewed as a customer computing system that they do not own. IaaS requires organizations to be able to hire the necessary people with broad computing expertise. IaaS customers will be responsible for all security aspects of the systems they use except physical security, which will be handled by the cloud provider. IaaS is also known as Hardware as a Service (HaaS).[55]

---

[54] Toni Mastelic, et. al. (2014). Cloud Computing: Survey on Energy Efficiency. *ACM Computing Surveys, Vol. 47, No. 2, Article 33.*

[55] S. Srinivasan (2014). *Cloud Computing Basics.* (New York: Springer), p. 10. See also: Nick Antonopoulos and Lee Gillam, Eds. (2010). *Cloud Computing. Principles, Systems and*

Platform as a Service (PaaS) provides customers with a platform, such as a Windows operating system, with the server capacity needed to run applications for customers. The cloud service provider PaaS manages the system for maintenance and provision of its tools such as .NET and Java whereas the customer is responsible for the selection of applications running on their platform of choice using the available tools. So, it is customers are responsible for the security challenges associated with the applications they use.[56]

Software as a Service (SaaS) provides server hardware and software to an organization without any complications in managing IT systems. The simplest example of a SaaS service is email for an organization. Cloud providers benefit from economies of scale in managing large infrastructure due to their strengths in that area and being able to provide the required computing resources to users who are mostly SMEs at an affordable cost. SaaS leaves complete control of the computing

---

Applications. (London: Springer), p. 4-5; Derrick Rountree (2014). *Op cit,* p. 25.

[56] S. Srinivasan (2014), *Op cit,* p. 10; Nick Antonopoulos and Lee Gillam, Eds. (2010), p. 4.

system to the provider. Some of the big SaaS providers are Amazon, Google, Microsoft, and SalesForce. SaaS is the most widely used cloud computing service today.[57]

In addition to the types of services mentioned above, there are also other types of services, namely: Storage as a Service (StaaS), Security as a Service (SecaaS), Data as a Service (DaaS), and Testing as a Service (TaaS).[58] Storage as a Service (StaaS) is a business model where cloud providers provide cloud space rentals for storage on their own infrastructure. In this model the StaaS provider will usually sign a Service Level Agreement (SLA) with businesses that require automatic back up and direct data transfer into their storage systems. SLAs are required by users to guarantee good and continuous service and to get replacement or compensation if the service is interrupted. Security as a Service (SecaaS), an important model that has great potential for success. Under this model companies that do not have adequate expertise in the field of security management can outsource security aspects.

---

[57] S. Srinivasan (2014), *supra,* p. 9; Nick Antonopoulos and Lee Gillam, Eds. (2010), p. 5; Derrick Rountree (2014). *Op cit.* p. 25.

[58] S. Srinivasan (2014), *Op cit,* p. 11.

Typical applications in this regard are the deployment of Anti-virus software and network monitoring. This service will benefit more small and medium-sized companies as they lack the necessary expertise to manage security for their data.[59] Data as a Service (DaaS). The basic premise of this model is to generate timely information by processing various data stored in text, images, sound, and video forms. Most of this data is generated by social media. For example, combining the position information shared by social network users with the time of day gives advertisers the ability to target the right market to the right audience for their goods. Testing as a Service (TaaS) is a model that tries to emulate what is already quite successful in industrial applications. Companies that develop a specific product as part of a larger development process get the product tested by a third-party company with expertise in the field. This helps the company to continue to focus on its core strengths and at the same time get secondary products to market. This type of service is ideal for cloud computing when the item being tested is a new software product and not a physical device.

---

[59] *Op cit,* p. 12.

Despite many efforts to improve cloud computing performance, there are still some obstacles that must be overcome. For example, scalability issues must be addressed by integrating high-performance platforms and techniques to improve computing and data storage performance.

In addition, there are security and privacy problems about distributed denial of service (DDOS) as well as phishing attacks, which considered as the biggest challenge to the widespread use of cloud computing services by users and customers. In fact, phishing has become a complex and increasing threat to Internet security, because just by gathering a small amount of information about the victim, attackers can generate a fully personalized email. These phishers are also not easy to catch, as most of them can hide their server location and work in complete anonymity. Even users with excellent security software can become victim to phishing attacks, as for the most part they rely entirely on information typed into forms, not considering malware infection on the computer.[60]

Due to data security issues that are always a concern in the use of cloud computing. For that there is an integrated security framework created for cloud businesses. The framework features multiple layers of security along with large-scale penetration testing and experiments to validate its robustness and effectiveness. They provide proof-of-concepts and lessons that are critical to the security of Big Data in the cloud, as follows: First, it ensures that all cloud services are safe and secure, including data in and out of data centers hosted on hundreds and thousands of virtual machines (VMs). Second, it also ensures that large amounts of data and Big Data can be safely processed and analyzed in the cloud and explains the need for large-scale penetration testing to validate the security framework.[61]

---

[60] Ike Vayansky and Sathish Kumar (2018). Phishing – challenges and solutions, article *in* Computer Fraud & Security - January 2018.

[61] Victor Chang, *et. al* (2016). Cloud computing adoption framework: A security framework for business clouds. *Future Generation Computer Systems 57 (2016) 24–41.*

In the field of data security, a cloud computing adoption framework (CCAF) layered security system has been developed, which has three levels of cloud security that can be applied to private and public clouds, namely: (i) *Access Control and Firewall*. Security at this level is supported by password protection (password), access control mechanisms, and firewall protection; (ii) *Intrusion Detection System (IDS) and Intrusion Prevention System (IPS)*. This is to detect attacks, intrusions, and penetrations, and prevent attacks, such as denial of service (DoS), antispoofing, port scanning, pattern-based attacks, parameter tampering, cross-site scripting, injection SQL, and cookie poisoning; and (iii) *Encryption/Decryption Control*. This level is supported by encryption and decryption of files and messages, including security controls. This feature monitors the system and provides an early warning once a detailed entity begins to behave abnormally.[62]

With the three levels of data security developed for cloud computing, it is hoped that users will no longer hesitate to use these computing services. Even though it

---

[62] Victor Chang, *et. al* (2016), *Op cit.*

has been equipped with multiple layers of security, it will not be able to prevent or inhibit the possibility of crimes such as hacker attacks, data destruction and theft. If that happens, the legal problem that arises is regarding the liability of cloud computing providers to their clients who use the cloud as a place to store data. For this reason, it is necessary to pay attention to the importance of a cloud usage agreement that is equipped with a provider liability clause in the event of hackers' attack, data destruction or data theft.

Big Data

The term Big Data refers to the set of digital data from a variety of digital sources, including sensors, digitizers, scanners, numerical modeling, cell phones, the Internet, video, email, and social networks. The types of data collected also vary, including text, geometry, images, video, sound, and combination of all of them.[63]

---

[63] Chaowei Yang, *et. al.* (2017) Big Data and cloud computing: innovation opportunities and challenges. *International Journal of Digital Earth, 10:1, 13-53.*

In Latin, 'dare' which later changed to 'data' means 'to give' something, that is, everything that is obtained from a situation. Then the use of the word 'dare', turns into something that is taken in various ways, for example something obtained through observation, processing, experimentation, and from notes.

Actually the more appropriate word for this is not 'dare' but 'capere' which later turns into 'capta' which comes from the Latin which means 'to take', which is something that has been selected and taken from the total potential available. Therefore, it may be an oddity that it is generally accepted that the name used to designate a unit in science is 'datum' instead of 'captum'. In fact, science is not concerned with what nature has given to scientists, but with what scientists have taken from nature according to what is required.[64]

Since 2011, interest in Big Data has grown rapidly. In contrast to most computer science research, Big Data has received significant attention from various media. News

---

[64] Colin Strong (2015). Humanizing Big Data: Marketing at the Meeting of Data, Social Science and Consumer Insight. (London: Kogan Page Limited), p. 21.

about Big Data and its goodness and the possibility of invasion of privacy has been a topic in various media and talk about Big Data since the beginning related to technology technical and socio-technical issues but until now the exact definition remains unclear. There are so many sources that the definitions are ambiguous and often contradictory.[65]

However, Microsoft provides a succinct definition: 'Big Data is an increasingly used term to describe the process of applying the latest serious computing power in machine learning and artificial intelligence to extremely massive data and dozens of extremely complex information sets.'[66]

But in its development Big Data terminology has become something universal. However, because it comes from various sources, namely academia, industry and the

---

[65] Jonathan Stuart Ward and Adam Barker. Undefined By Data: A Survey of Big Data Definitions. School of Computer Science. University of St Andrews, UK.

[66] The Big Bang: How the Big Data Explosion Is Changing the World - Microsoft UK Enterprise Insights Blog - Site Home - MSDN Blogs. http://blogs.msdn.com/b/microsoft enterprise insight/archive/2013/04/15/the-big-bang-how-the-big-data-explosion-is-changing-the-world.aspx.

media, there is no uniform definition, besides that, all parties who are stakeholders provide different definitions and even contradict each other. One of the definitions given by the leading ICT consulting firm Gartner is:

> *"Big data is high volume, high velocity, and/or high variety information assets that require new forms of processing to enable enhanced decision making, insight discovery and process optimization."[67]*

This lack of a uniform definition causes confusion and hinders the general discussion of Big Data. But in general, the characteristics of Big Data are: Volume (amount) is very large usually the total size of data in terabytes and above; Velocity (growth) of data is very fast, the data increases in very large quantities in a short period of time; and Variety (various forms or data formats), it can be data in plain text files, database tables such as MySQL, Excel files or any form. Although some parties add two other "Vs", namely Veracity (data accuracy and processing results) and Value (value

---

[67] Michael Wigley (2016). *Big Data: Are Lawyers Screwed (And What to Do About Big Data Until Then)?* Wellington: Wigley and Company, June 2016.

generated by the data), the above definition is sufficient to show the form of Big Data in general.[68]

The specialty of Big Data is that it can work with both structured data and unstructured data. For structured data, such as spreadsheets, timesheets, and so on: which is already organized, it is relatively easy to manage to turn it into information that has value. For unstructured data, such as emails, videos, etc., millions of emails, for example, are relatively more difficult to process to get useful results. However, it can now be handled using the rapidly evolving Big Data technology. The challenge faced today is no longer about how to get the data, but how to get the right and useful data.

In general, the data collected consists of several types of data, namely: Structured data: Data that consists of types that already have a certain format, and structure (for example, transaction data, online analytical processing [OLAP] data, traditional RDBMS data, CSV files, as well as simple spreadsheets); Semi-structured data: Textual

---

[68] Jonathan Stuart Ward and Adam Barker. Undefined By Data: A Survey of Big Data Definitions. United Kingdom: School of Computer Science University of St Andrews.

data files with visible patterns that allow for analysis (such as Extensible Markup Language [XML] data files that can be parsed and described by XML skimming); Quasi-structured data: Incorrectly formatted textual data that can be reformatted with effort, equipment, and time (for example, click-through data from the web which may be inconsistent in value and data format); and Unstructured data: Data that does not have a specific structure, which may be text files, PDFs, images, and videos. [69]

Various authorities including financial authorities have defined the big data phenomenon as a collection of various factors, including the collection of data that is available everywhere and from various sources, the cost of data storage is likely to fall and the capacity to analyze data is getting stronger.[70]

---

[69] Nancy Gessler and Alok Shrivastava. Eds. (2015). *Data Science & Big Data Analytics: Discovering, Analyzing, Visualizing and Presenting Data*. (Indianapolis: John Wiley & Sons, Inc), p. 6.

[70] U.S. Federal Trade Commission Report, January (2016,), "Big Data: A tool for Inclusion or Exclusion?" January, p. 1; EBA, EIOPA and ESMA (2016), "European Joint Committee Discussion Paper on the Use of Big Data by Financial Institutions," JC 2016 86, p. 7.

Data is collected from various sources. Currently, everyone and everything leaves a digital footprint. The sources of Big Data generated by new applications and the scale and rate of data growth, generate scalable volumes of data at scale, provide opportunities for new analytics and drive new value for many. Data can come from various sources, ranging from medical information, such as genome sequencing and diagnostic imaging, photos and video recordings to mobile phones and surveillance videos.[71]

Big Data collection involves a distributed computing environment and massively parallel processing (MPP) architecture, which is a way of processing large amounts of data by distributing processing across hundreds or thousands of processors, which may be run in the same place or on separate computers located far from each other, allowing absorption and the parallel data analysis approach used to process such complex data.[72]

---

[71] Nancy Gessler and Alok Shrivastava. Eds. (2015). *Op cit,* p. 16.
[72] *Op cit*, p. 5.

Generally, the data has the following characteristics: Personal data (proprietary data), open data, creative commons data, and public domain data. In general, the data collected is in the form of data that has or is subject to copyright, database rights, moral rights, trademark rights, and rights to trade secrets or confidential information, all of which relate to various applicable laws and regulations.

The process of collecting and forming Big Data consists of two main parts: data management and data analysis.

Data Management

Data management is a process consists of three stages:

Acquisition and recording

At this stage there are several things that must be considered, given the very fast and extraordinary growth in data acquisition. In smart city concept, for example, sensors electronically connected to a common platform to make collecting and analyzing the resulting data simple. Data acquisition is accelerating, in comparison when the human genome was first decoded in 2003, it took almost ten years to sequence as many as 3.2 billion genome pairs from one person. Now a single device can sequence a person's complete genome in just a few hours. The collection and use of personal data raise privacy concerns, such as misuse of data. Although the data can also be used to save lives or make life better, or maybe even safer.[73]

Data acquisition can be done in various ways, one of which is by using sensors. Sensors are found in many devices used in everyday life by everyone, including mobile devices, which are currently used in various environments, such as smartphones (smartphones), smartwatches (smart watches), smart bracelets, tablets, and medical sensors.[74] Sensor types can also be distinguished from the purpose of the sensor, the working environment and the type of data obtained. The

---

[73] Ivan Miguel Pires (2015). From Data Acquisition to Data Fusion: A Comprehensive Review and a Roadmap for the Identification of Activities of Daily Living Using Mobile Devices. *Sensors 2016, 16, 184.*

[74] Ivan Miguel Pires (2015). *Op cit.*

environment itself can be classified as controlled, uncontrolled, static, dynamic, uncertain, and undefined.[75]

Advances in communication technology, computing, digital sensors, and data storage support the rise of the Big Data era. Digital data can be collected from many sources, including from customer order transaction data, from emails and attachments, from radio frequency identification (RFID) sensors, and from smartphones (smartphones) in the form of films, video recordings, and audio recordings.[76]

In terms of data acquisition methods, data collection methods cover four groups, including those related to data collection, multisensory data, in the health sector for example data can be obtained from brain sensing and real time sensing. The data collection method also includes hidden approaches, for example: (i) *keystroke logger* and *clickstream* both of which can provide real-time insights into consumer behavior; (ii) *smart sensor* and RFID which are ubiquitous, such as in devices, products,

---

[75] Muhammad Shoaib, et. al. (2014). Fusion of Smartphone Motion Sensors for Physical Activity Recognition. *Sensors 2014, 14, 10146-10176; doi:10.3390/s140610146.*
[76] Ivan Miguel Pires (2015). *Op cit.*

buildings, and even installed around cities; (iii) health monitors for humans and animals in monitoring body temperature, blood pressure, etc.; (iv) drone sensors including ornithopters for flapping wings and cameras for photographing the size of a postage stamp; and (v) samples from metamaterials that directly compress images and scenes, eliminating the need for post-capture processing.[77]

Now with multi sensor data devices, terabytes of Big Data can be obtained using only video surveillance cameras from surveillance cameras and traffic monitoring or coast guard cameras and data acquisition can also be done using ordinary mobile devices. The advantage of using mobile devices for data acquisition is related to the possibility of obtaining data anywhere and anytime because mobile devices can be carried anywhere.

However, there are some limitations in data acquisition performance for real-time applications, namely the multitasking execution pattern which will

---

[77] James M. TIEN (2013). BIG DATA: UNLEASHING INFORMATION. *J Syst Sci Syst Eng (Jun 2013) 22(2): 127-151.*

differ between different mobile devices, as it depends on processing capabilities, memory and power capabilities, which are very limited, as well as limitations and on the system operations as well as on the number and types of mobile applications currently available.[78] But by looking at the progress made in the field of technology, it is possible that in the near future this problem can be overcome.

Extraction, Cleaning and Annotation

Data from the acquisition cannot be used immediately, because it is usually still in the form of 'raw' data and has not been compiled. For that data must be extracted, cleaned, and annotated. Extraction aims to retrieve data that is truly relevant from the overall data obtained. Data cleaning is to deal with lost data by identifying tampering and to eliminate, as well as to resolve inconsistencies.[79]

Data quality is important for data users. To measure the quality of data, an examination of the accuracy,

---

[78] Ivan Miguel Pires (2015). *Op cit.*

[79] Ronald Fagin, et. al. (2016). Declarative Cleaning of Inconsistencies in Information Extraction. *ACM Transactions on Database Systems, Vol. 41, No. 1, Article 6.*

completeness, consistency, timeliness, trustworthiness, and interpretability of the data is carried out. Accuracy is about whether the data is correct or not, accurate or not, while completeness is related to the problem of how to record data.

Consistency, related to the issue of whether the data has been sorted and changed whether some data has not been sorted and changed. Timeliness of data is about whether the data is updated on time and changes and with the same frequency. Interpretability is a description of how easy the data is to understand, because it often happens that in use, a data is incomplete with its attributes or lacks value, or only contains global aggregate data which can lead to incomplete results. After the process is executed, then the cleaned data is annotated, and indexed so that it easy to access and manipulate data.[80]

The process of data extraction, data cleaning, data integration, data transformation, and data reduction can be considered as the preprocessing process of data analysis carried out to extract useful data from raw data

---

[80] Lillian Pierson (2017). *Data Science For Dummies®, 2nd Edition*. Hoboken, New Jersey: John Wiley & Sons, Inc.

(also known as primary data) and refine it so that it can be used for further analysis. If the data obtained is a copy or duplicate, incomplete, inconsistent, unclear, or questionable, then this process will clean it up. If the data is too complex or too large to handle, this process will also try to reduce it. If the raw data has errors or is incomplete, in this process it will be identified and made to be consistent.[81]

Integration, Aggregation and Representation

The data integration is a process carried out to link separate data sources to provide valuable and actionable data values based on these interconnected data. Aggregated surveillance data of individual homes can be collected again in the cloud to analyze the security of the area. While on the device itself, data aggregation serves as a pillar of the application workflow, and directly affects the quality of the software system.[82]

---

[81] Chun-Wei Tsai, *et. al*. Big Data Analytics: A Survey. *Journal of Big Data (2015) 2:21.*

[82] Simin Cai, *et.al.* (2019). Data aggregation processes: a survey, a taxonomy, and design guidelines. *Computing (2019) 101:1397–1429.*

Data can be aggregated by category, usually determined in the order of groups from the results of data collection. For example, in a temporal database, users can choose to aggregate data by day, week, or month, with a more granular breakdown; in a spatial database, aggregations can be based on roads, cities, and provinces. In the database, the stored data usually has many dimensions, and merging can be done on various dimensions. Often, data needs to be retrieved from multiple data sources through extraction, transformation, and loading processes, which aim to extract, validate, and normalize the raw data prior to aggregation.[83]

Data Representation refers to the methods used to represent information stored in a computer or in the cloud. Data and instructions cannot be entered and processed directly into a computer using human language. Each type of data, numbers, letters, special symbols, sounds or images must first be converted into machine-readable form, namely binary form. Therefore, it is necessary to understand how computers and their peripheral devices

---

[83] Simin Cai, *et.al.* (2019). *Op cit.*

handle data in electronic circuits, also about storage in magnetic media and in optical devices.[84]

Computer devices and cloud computing technology can store many different types of information: unconnected information such as numbers and letters, or continuous information such as sounds and images. One method is storage by using a numeric code to represent the data, in which information stored in a series of zeros and ones known as a binary code.[85]

In a binary system, electronic components, such as microprocessors, which consist of millions of electronic circuits, the availability of high voltage (on) in the circuit is defined as '1' while low voltage (off) is defined as '0'. In practice, a binary code is preferred over other codes (e.g., ternary code) for two reasons: **(i)** The maximum advantage over the effects of noise in a transmission medium is obtained by using a binary code, because a

---

[84] See for example: Ron White (2015). *How Computers Work, Tenth Edition*. Indianapolis: QUE.
[85] Simon Haykin and Michael Moher (2007). *Introduction to Analog and Digital Communications. Second Edition.* (Hoboken, NJ: John Wiley & Sons, Inc.), p. 148.

binary symbol withstands a relatively high level of noise; (ii) The binary code is easy to generate and regenerate.[86]

Data Analysis

The analysis of data, especially high-volume data, depends on the suitability of the abstract description of the data, that is, the suitability of the data schema that the analysis tool can process. It is concerned with the correct identification of the nature of the data and is very important for the success of data analysis.

Data analysis is an activity to obtain and evaluate the extracted data into useful information. Data analysis simply covers several concepts such as 'Big data', 'data integration', 'data mining' and 'data matching'.[87]

The database schema clearly demonstrates this trait, for example by marking sales figures, zip codes, locations, and the like. For decades, this data is taken from all kinds of applications and entered databases. The

---

[86] Simon Haykin and Michael Moher (2007). *Op cit.,* p. 209.
[87] Australian Government (2018). Guide to Data Analytics and the Australian Privacy Principles. Office of the Australian Information Commissioner.oaic.gov.au.

application used must be able to ensure that it will get all this data in a format suitable for the analysis tool.[88]

Data analysis consists of: (i) Descriptive analysis by analyzing past data to present it in a summary form that can be easily interpreted; (ii) Diagnostic analysis is the analysis of past data to diagnose the reasons for the occurrence of certain events; (iii) Predictive analysis is the prediction of the occurrence of an event or the possible outcome of an event or forecasting the future value using a predictive model; (iv) Prescriptive analysis is to predict various outcomes and the best course of action for each analysis result.[89] Data analysis consists of two stages: Data modelling and Data interpretation.

Data Modelling

The problem of large-scale data analysis did not appear suddenly but has existed for decades because

---

[88] Marcello Trovati, Richard Hill, Ashiq Anjum, Shao Ying Zhu, Lu Li, Eds (2015). *Big-Data Analytics and Cloud Computing. Theory, Algorithms and Applications.* (Switzerland: Springer International Publishing), p. 23.

[89] Arshdeep Bahga & Vijay Madisetti (2019). *Big Data Analytics: A Hands-On Approach.* Ebook - website: www.hands-on-books-series. com., p. 61.

collecting data is much easier than finding useful things from the data. Although today's computer systems are much faster than they were decades ago, large-scale data remains a difficult burden for today's computers to analyze. Advances in computer systems and internet technology have experienced the development of computing hardware for decades, but the problem of handling large-scale data still exists until today's Big Data era.[90]

To analyze the data collected in Big Data, the traditional data analysis methods developed for the centralized data analysis process cannot be applied directly to Big Data.

Proper data modeling and storage provides benefits and advantages for utilizing Big Data: (i) *Performance*: Good data modeling can help speed to perform required data searches and reduce overall Input/Output; (ii) *Cost*: Good data modeling can significantly reduce unnecessary data redundancy, reuse computational results, and reduce storage and compute costs for Big Data systems; (iii) *Efficiency*: Good data modeling greatly improves user

---

[90] Chun-Wei Tsai, *et. al. Op cit.*

experience and improves data usage efficiency; (iv) *Quality*: Good data modeling makes data statistics more consistent and reduces the possibility of computational errors.[91]

There are several methodologies that are often used for data modeling, namely:

Model Entity-Relationship (ER), data modeling that covers all company activities and can describe the company's business through modeling with the entity-relationship (ER) method. This type of ER modeling has three phases: (i) High-level modeling which describes the relationship between themes, used to describe the general picture of the company; (ii) Mid-level modeling to obtain detailed data and themes based on high-level models; (iii) Physical modeling operated with mid-level models to design physical characteristics according to physical storage availability, performance, and platform characteristics.[92]

[91] Alibaba Cloud. https://www.alibabacloud.com/blog/a-com parison-of-data-modeling-methods-for-big-data_593761. Accessed January 16, 2021.
[92] W.H. Inmon (2005). *Building the Data Warehouse, Fourth Edition*. (Indianapolis: Wiley Publishing, Inc.), p. 81-99.

Dimensional Modeling, deal with analytical decision making and needs analysis issues. Its primary focus is on enabling users to complete analysis quickly while maintaining high performance when handling large and complex queries. Model design includes the following steps: (i) Application selection which involves analysis and decision making. An application can be a single business event, such as issuing a refund, the state of an event, for example, an account balance or a process containing a series of interrelated events; (ii) Detail selection. In event analysis, we need to define the sub-division level for all analyzes first to determine the details. Granularity is a combination of dimensions. (iii) Identify the dimension table. After selecting a breakdown, design a dimension table based on the breakdown, including the dimension attributes. This table caters for grouping and filtering during analysis. (iv) Selection of facts. Decide which indicators you should measure during the analysis.[93]

---

[93] Ralph Kimball and Margy Ross (2013). *The Data Warehouse Toolkit: The Definitive Guide to Dimensional Modeling, Third Edition*. (Indianapolis: John Wiley & Sons, Inc), p. 37-49.

Data Vault Model, this model is useful for integrating data, but cannot be used directly for data analysis and decision making. The model emphasizes establishing an auditable underlying data layer with a focus on data history, traceability, and atomicity. This model does not require excessive processing or integration of consistency. This model allows the company data to be organized thematically, structured, and can also introduce further normal form processing to optimize the model so that it scales properly with changes to the source system. The Data Vault model consists of: (i) Hub: The company's core business entity, which consists of the entity key, data warehouse serial surrogate key, load time, and data source; (ii) Links: Links show connections between hubs. The biggest difference between the Data Vault Model and the ER Model is that relationships are abstracted as independent units, which increases the scalability of the model. It consists of a hub surrogate key, load time, and data source. (iii) Satellite: The satellite includes a detailed description of th e hub. One hub may have multiple satellites. The satellite consists of a hub replacement key, load time, source type, and a detailed hub description. [94]

Anchor Model, the core concept is that all extensions involve additions, not modifications. Therefore, it normalizes the model to 6NF, and it becomes a K-V structural model. The Anchor Model consists of: (i) Anchors: Anchors are like Hubs in the Vault Data Model. This model represents a business entity and only has a primary key; (ii) Attributes: Attributes are like satellites in the Data Warehouse Model but are more normalized. This model is in a K-V structure. Each table describes the attributes of only one anchor; (iii) Tie: Tie shows the relationship between Anchor and is explained using a table. Bonds are like links in the Data Warehouse Model and can increase the extensibility of the general model; (iv) Node: Node stands for attributes that may be shared by multiple anchors, for example, named and public attributes such as gender and country.[95]

---

[94] Daniel Linstedt and Michael Olschimke (2016). *Building a Scalable Data Warehouse with Data Vault 2.0*. (Oxford: Elsevier), p. 33-43.

[95] Lars. Rönnbäck. Anchor Modeling – Agile Information Modeling in Evolving Data Environments. http://www.

Data Interpretation

The final stage of data analysis is the data interpretation stage. Data interpretation or interpretation refers to the implementation of the process through which data is reviewed for the purpose of arriving at an informed conclusion. Data interpretation gives meaning to the analyzed information and determines its significance and implications. The importance of data interpretation has been proven in various data utilization therefore, it needs to be done in the right way.

Data is very likely to be collected from various sources and tends to enter the analysis process in an unordered and unstructured manner. Data interpretation is designed to assist in understanding the numerical data that has been collected, analyzed, and presented. To interpret the data required a structured basic method and a consistent foundation.[96]

anchormodeling.com/wp-content/uploads/2011/05/Anchor-Modeling.pdf. Accessed January 16, 2021.

[96] https://www.datapine.com/blog/data-interpretation-methods-benefits-problems. Accessed January 18, 2021.

Data interpretation is designed to help people understand the numerical data that has been collected, analyzed, and presented. Data interpretation designed to help people understand the numerical data that has been collected, analyzed, and presented. Data analysis and interpretation, regardless of qualitative/ quantitative methods and status, may include the following characteristics: identification and explanation of data; compare data; data identification; and predictions for the future.[97]

Data analysis and interpretation helps improve processes and identify problems. It is difficult to grow and make reliable improvements without data collection and interpretation. Unclear ideas about improving performance exist across all institutions and industries, but without proper research and analysis, an idea is likely to remain stagnant forever.[98]

In the era of Big Data, the challenge is no longer about getting the data, it's about getting the data right and about

---

[97] National Research Council. 2013. *Frontiers in Massive Data Analysis.* Washington, D.C.: The National Academies Press.
[98] *Op cit.*

using computers to add to existing knowledge and identify patterns that were not seen or could not find before.[99] Big data is worthless in storage, because the value of the data is not in the data itself but in the purpose for which the data is used. Data is a strategic asset. But data only has value if it is used constructively and appropriately to get good results.

For companies and analytical entities, using large amounts of data can prove to be a profitable value proposition.[100] Its potential value emerges, for example, when it is used to assist decision making. To enable data-driven decision-making, efficient processes are needed to turn high-volume, fast-moving, and diverse data into meaningful insights. This means that technologies that allow for storing, processing, and analyzing large amounts of data will continue to increase in use.

In conclusion, the whole process of extracting and collecting big data can be divided into five stages. These five stages form two main sub-processes: data

---

[99] Jared Dean (2014). *Big data, data mining, and machine learning: value creation for business leaders and practitioners.* (New Jersey: John Wiley & Sons, Inc.), p. 5.
[100] *Op cit,* p. 12.

management and data analysis. Data management involves processes and supporting technologies for obtaining and storing data and for preparing and retrieving it for analysis. Data analysis, on the other hand, refers to the techniques used to analyze and derive information from big data. Thus, big data analysis can be seen as a sub-process in the whole big data extraction process.[101]

The last two decades have fundamentally changed the way data is handled. Every day more and more data are generated. This emerging data is not a waste product but is a hidden treasure waiting to be discovered by curious and motivated researchers and practitioners who see this trend and are eager to reach out to meet the challenges of the future.[102]

Big Data obtained from social media, Facebook, Twitter, LinkedIn, and others can be used by processing the data together with business data from a company, for example customer data that already exists in the company

---

[101] A. Gandomi, M. Haider. Beyond the hype: big data concepts, methods, and analytics. *International Journal of Information Management 35 (2015), pp. 137–144.*
[102] Ivan Miguel Pires (2015). *Op cit,* p. 8.

database or product sales data, etc., Big Data then processed for the purpose of preparing a marketing plan for company product.

Big Data is used by businesses for a variety of purposes, classic examples of data usage being Uber and its taxis, and Amazon and its bookstores, where Uber analyzes and utilizes large amounts of information to provide services to individual consumers. Similarly, Amazon analyzes millions of data to be able to recommend a book that is the best read for its consumers.[103]

In practice, the use of such data is often not with the permission of the data owner, especially regarding personal data, the consent for the use of data is usually only stated in the terms and conditions when someone is about to sign-up to a certain service provider. for example, Facebook, Twitter, Yahoo (e-mail) and others.

Big Data is at the heart of the revolution in all fields that use 'smart' frills. The basic idea behind the phrase 'Big Data' is that everything that is done will leave a digital footprint (or data), which can be used and analyzed to

---

[103] Michael Wigley (2016). *Op cit.*

become smarter. The driving force in this new, more advanced world is access to ever-increasing volumes of data and the ever-increasing ability of technology to mine that data for commercial purposes. Every industry is actively learning to benefit from Big Data analytics, and seems confident that by collecting, recording, and analyzing data they will find innovative methods to play a big business role in the future.[104]

The ability to use Big Data is shown in the form of various smart applications that make it easy for people both in the economy and business, as well as in everyday life, such as in smart home applications, smart cities, and various smart applications in the economic and business fields.

In addition, Big Data is also used for law enforcement and prevention of violations, now the police investigation department has used smart technology to reduce the number of crimes and reduce the threat of crime.

---

[104] Bernard Marr (2015). *Big data: Using Smart Big Data, Analytics and Metrics to Make Better Decisions and Improve Performance*. (West Sussex: John Wiley & Sons Ltd.), p. 9.

For example, in London currently installed about 422,000 CCTV cameras that can record the movements of a person suspected of being a criminal. This video camera can be routinely used to create a 3D (three-dimensional) face image of a suspect which can then be compared with facial photos on the internet or on social media. If the suspect has a profile photo on his Facebook account, the images obtained from CCTV will be identified using facial recognition technology. In the future investigators will be able to find out all information about a suspect, with just a photo or a snippet from a video.[105] This installation of surveillance cameras is reminiscent of the 'Big Brother' surveillance in George Orwell's "1984."

Law enforcement is constantly looking for ways to use technology and Big Data to fight crime. In Silicon Valley, biometric technology is being used to create weapons that will only fire when used by a person authorized to shoot. CCTV cameras are no longer just observers who stay and helpless in one place, now

---

[105] Barrett, D. (2013) 'One surveillance camera for every 11 people in Britain, says CCTV survey', *The Telegraph.* Cited by Bernard Marr (2015), *Op cit,* p. 130.

86

cameras are commonly used in police cars and police
bodies to take permanent digital video recordings of
everything that happens around them and are also
connected to drones that controlled by remote control.[106]
Installing cameras in cars and on police bodies has proven
to make it easier to prove cases, as was the case with the
death of a policeman arrested in Minneapolis, and the
recent shooting of a teenager by a police officer.[107]

In the use of Big Data, there are legal issues related to
the security of personal data, legal protection of data, and
use by other parties, as well as by the social media
providers. These matters will be discussed further to
determine whether the existing statutory instruments are
adequate or whether there is a need for additional
statutory instruments.

Legal problems have started to arise since the data
acquisition process, namely questions about ownership

---

[106] Bernard Marr (2015), *Op cit,* p. 131.
[107] The case of the murder of George Floyd on May 25, 2020,
which caused massive protests almost all over the world, is
evident in the video footage from the cameras on the police
surrounding him. Likewise, the shooting of Daunte Wright on
April 12, 2021, was caught on camera by the policeman who
shot him.

and protection of data, which related to personal information that has been obtained. In addition, data acquisition also raises questions about the contractual relationship if the data is sold and purchased, including regarding the buyer's rights in the event of a breach of contract if after delivery it turns out that the data is damaged, or the data sent is inaccurate or of lower quality than promised between the parties.[108]

Regarding data ownership, questions arise about the importance of the data, for example about the legal or illegal ownership by an owner and user of a smart car: first, the data generated by the car may contain information about the behavior and location of the driver in certain situations. This information can enable conclusions to be drawn as to whether the person behind the wheel is generally a cautious or risky driver, or whether the car was at the scene of a crime. Given the sensitivity of this information, it is self-evident that the

---

[108] Nikolaus Forgó, Stefanie Hänold and Benjamin Schütze (2017). *The Principle of Purpose Limitation and Big Data* in Marcelo Corrales, Mark Fenwick, Nikolaus Forgó, *Eds* (2017). *New Technology, Big Data, and the Law. Perspectives in Law, Business, and Innovation.* (Singapore: Springer), p. 21.

driver of the car concerned has an important interest in limiting the use of the information.[109]

Second, the owner must have a legitimate interest in extracting value from data about the functioning of the car's technical components and their environment, such as road conditions, weather, and traffic. To collect and transmit this data, the car needs to be operated, which means someone must drive the vehicle and pay for fuel or electricity. As a result, it is natural for the owner, who normally bears these costs, to have the right to "sell" the operating data.[110]

The manufacturer of a smart device is also a stakeholder in the IoT concept. Especially, regarding the data that is directly attached to the device. For a car manufacturer, for example, data on the long-term performance of car components, as well as the average characteristics of their customers, will be very important in terms of substantial product improvement. In addition, some of the information that can be obtained from this

---

[109] Christoph Kronke (2018). Data regulations on the internet of things. Frontiers of Law in China, 13(3), 367-379.
[110] Christoph Kronke (2018). *Op cit.*

data may include trade secrets, which are clearly the legitimate interests of the manufacturer. The manufacturer may be interested in developing entirely new functions and products to complement the car, or at least selling the data to third parties who may develop such complementary products or use the data otherwise.[111]

Until now, legal issues regarding data ownership are still not very clear, in some countries it is still a debate whether data can become property rights like ownership rights over other objects. In the UK, when the Court of Appeals had to decide whether data was subject to liens, i.e., a person's right to remain in the possession of another person's property until the owner resolved a claim by the owner, the Court concluded that despite compelling arguments for extending the use of liens to digital materials, The court stated that the existing laws and regulations could not be interpreted in such a way. The

---

[111] *Ibid.*

court concluded that it should be left to legislators to expand the law to include digital material.[112]

In Indonesian legislation, the term Big Data is not yet known, but in general the data has been contained in the Information and Electronic Transactions Act:

> Article 1.1
> Electronic Information is one or a set of electronic data, including but not limited to writing, sound, images, maps, designs, photographs, electronic data interchange (EDI), electronic mail (electronic mail), telegram, telex, telecopy or the like, letters, processed signs, numbers, Access Codes, symbols, or perforations that have meaning or can be understood by people who are able to understand them.

Likewise, in Government Regulation Number 82 of 2012 the same definition is stated.

> Article 1.6
> Electronic Information is one or a set of electronic data, including but not limited to writing, sound, images, maps, designs, photographs, electronic data interchange (EDI), electronic mail (electronic mail), telegram, telex,

---

[112] Christine Storr and Pam Storr (2017). Internet of Things: Right to Data from a European Perspective in Marcelo Corrales, Mark Fenwick, Nikolaus Forgó, *Eds* (2017). *New Technology, Big Data, and the Law. Perspectives in Law, Business, and Innovation.* (Singapore: Springer), p. 74.

telecopy or the like, letters, processed numbers, access codes, symbols, or perforatio that have meaning or can be understood by people who are able to understand them.

From the two provisions above, [electronic] data is part of electronic information, regardless of how big or small the data is (volume), its speed of increase (velocity), and its variety of forms (variety), so it can be said that Big Data has also been included in both these provisions.

Social Media

Since its inception in the 1960s, the Internet has been designed to be both a way of building logical networks and as a way of bringing together all the disparate networks and enabling them to function independently, i.e., as a building block and as the glue of linking the blocks. The internet is also built open to all types of devices, whether in the form of computers or other processors that can be part of this new network if they can be connected through interfaces and can run the minimum technical process requirements.

This principle and the protocol for its application have not changed since the Internet consists of only two connected terminals with a number that has exceeded hundreds of millions of people in both developed and developing countries.[113]

Development of social media

The openness of networks and Internet protocols opens the possibility for various devices to connect with each other, among which the most widely used until now is the cellular phone device which has now evolved from a device that was originally only used primarily for conducting conversations and sending short messages, into a mobile phone. computing devices that allow people to communicate with one another and provide information around the clock.

Smartphone devices have now turned into a kind of personal assistant that helps for almost everything, from finding the location of shops, hotels, and restaurants, as

---

[113] Jonathan L. Zittrain (2006). The Generative Internet. *Harvard Law Review, May 2006, Vol. 119, No. 7 (May 2006), pp. 1974-2040.* Citing: Neil Randall, Living Internet, ARPANET - The First Internet, http://livinginternet.com; Barry M. Leiner, *et al.* (1997). The Past and Future History of the Internet, COMM. ACM, Feb. 1997; and Brian E. Carpenter (1996). Architectural Principles of the Internet. http://www.ietf.org/ rfc/rfcI958.

well as for monitoring health, watching videos and shopping via the Internet.[114]

The development of smartphones is interrelated with the growth and development of social media. Because with easy access via smartphones, people are free to use social media. Social media such as Facebook has penetrated all sectors of society, especially among young people.[115] In addition, this social media has also become access to the Internet for beginners who access it for the first time. In developed countries such as the United States, 84% of online young adults (18-29 years) have used Facebook.[116]

Facebook was soon followed by various other types of social media such as Twitter, Instagram, Whatsapp, and others. Kietzman, et. al. stated that Twitter is an

---

[114] Nayeem Islam & Roy Want (2014). Smartphones: Past, Present, and Future. *Pervasive computing October–December 2014.* Published by the IEEE CS.

[115] Duggan, M., & Smith, A. (2013). Social media update 2013. Washington, DC: Pew Internet and American Life Project, in Teresa Correa (2016). Digital skills and social media use: how Internet skills are related to different types of Facebook use among 'digital natives.' *Information, Communication & Society, 19:8, 1095-1107.*

[116] *Op cit.*

example of social media that uses mobile devices and network-based technologies to create a highly interactive platform with which individuals as well as the public can share, co-create, discuss, and modify content created by social media users themselves.[117]

Now there are various types of social media from various providers and various countries. In 2021, there are 4.20 billion social media users worldwide. This number represents a growth of 490 million over a 12-month period, an increase of 13 percent annually. The number of social media users is 53 percent of the total world population.[118]

Impacts of social media

The development of social media has an impact on life, both positive and negative impacts. The positive impacts of social media include: (i) that social media helps people to stay connected to each other; (ii) provides useful information that can be sent via social networking

---

[117] J.H. Kietzmann, *et. al.* (2011). Social media? Get serious! Understanding the functional building blocks of social media. *Business Horizons 54 (3) (2011) 241–251.*
[118] Simon Kemp (2021). Digital 2021. Global Overview Report. Data reportal 27 January 2021.

sites; (iii) allows people to get online support that they may lack in conventional relationships; (iv) children can also get the information and advice they need through social media; (v) even people can use social media for things related to their career.[119] Negative impact of social media could be as follows: (i) that it becomes unclear who is the 'stranger' on social media; kidnapping, murder, robbery can be carried out using detailed personal data posted on social media; (ii) many cases are reported at police stations where adults targeting children and lure them into meeting; (iii) in addition, many young people waste their time on social sites such as chatting which also affects their health; (iv) there are also useless blogs that can influence young people so that they can turn violent and take inappropriate actions.[120]

Use of social media in business

In subsequent developments, social media has also changed the company's business procedures related to

---

[119] Shabnoor Siddiqui and Tajinder Singh (2016). Social Media its Impact with Positive and Negative Aspects. *International Journal of Computer Applications Technology and Research Volume 5– Issue 2, 71 - 75*, p. 74-75.

[120] Simon Kemp (2021). *Op cit.*

markets and society, creating new possibilities and opportunities in all aspects of the company from marketing, finance, and human resource management. The shift towards social media occurred in the Web 2.0 era, which is the second phase of Internet use in business, after the 'Dotcom bubble' era.

In the revival of the Internet business after the Dotcom bubble, the view is no longer solely aimed at the use of the Internet network but has begun to shift to the use of social media with various experiments on connectivity between e-commerce and social media. In the era of Web 2.0, the development of the use of social media in various company activities began to appear.[121]

In addition to carrying out marketing and product sales, in companies, social media also has the potential to support the transformation of knowledge and expertise exchange. Research shows that social media features can have a very strong impact and in time will have a major

---

[121] Tadhg Nagle & Andrew Pope (2013). Understanding Social Media Business Value. A Prerequisite for Social Media Selection. *Journal of Decision Systems, 22:4, 283-297.*

impact on product use and income for individuals and society at large.[122]

The potential use of social media in business can be seen from how quickly the content that is published gets a wider public response. An example can be seen in what happened to Twitter in 2014, when Ellen DeGeneres hosted the 2014 Academy Awards prize giving, she took selfies with Hollywood celebrities including Bradley Copper, using a Samsung Galaxy Note 3 smartphone. Ellen then posted the selfie on Twitter and captioned it: "If only Bradley's arm was longer. Best photo ever. #oscars". Ellen's tweet immediately went viral, receiving over 1.3 million retweets and causing the Twitter service to be interrupted for more than 20 minutes. By the end of the year, the selfie had received 3.3 million retweets from 151 countries. This made the Twitter post known as "the most retweeted tweet for the year 2014". And in that incident the Samsung Galaxy Note 3 received a kind of

---

[122] Sinan Aral, Chrysanthos Dellarocas and David Godes (2013). Introduction to the Special Issue: Social Media and Business Transformation: A Framework for Research. *Information Systems Research, March 2013, Vol. 24, No. 1, Special Issue on Social Media and Business Transformation (March 2013), pp. 3-13.*

product exposure that is unimaginable using traditional promotional channels.[123]

The use of social media is not only limited to business-to-consumer (B2C) relationships, but also includes business-to-business (B2B) relationships. Social media has a strong role to play in driving B2B engagement, especially as seen from a supplier's perspective, social media is an excellent tool to attract clients' attention and then create real business relationships.

However, while most suppliers want more active engagement with their buyers and other stakeholders through social media, the level of activity is below their expectations. While suppliers welcome some buyers, who show their support by 'like', or leaving comments, and sharing some content, the nature of engagement experienced in B2B interactions suggests a pattern of

---

[123] Clyde W. Holsapple, *et. al*. (2018). Business social media analytics: Characterization and conceptual framework. *Decision Support Systems 110 (2018) 32–45.*

passivity. Suppliers still see the benefits of using social media that come from the content on the social media.[124]

The use of social media in business is not without its obstacles. The biggest obstacle from outside the company is that most companies do not view social media as relevant to the company's industry. In addition, companies operating in traditional and restricted industries, such as the pharmaceutical industry, are less likely to use social media than companies operating in innovative industries, such as the technology industry. Furthermore, the company's internal barriers to the use of social media come from the ignorance of human resources in the field of sales and the absence of special training for the use of social media to support their role.[125]

---

[124] Jun Luo, *et. al.* (2021). Social media-related tensions on business-to-business markets – Evidence from China. *Industrial Marketing Management 93 (2021) 293–306.*

[125] Keith E. Niedermeier and Emily Wang (2016). The use of social media among business-to-business sales professionals in China. How social media helps create and solidify *guanxi* relationships between sales professionals and customers. *Journal of Research in Interactive Marketing Vol. 10 No. 1, 2016 pp. 33-49.*

Just as the development of the Internet is prone to use for crime and lawlessness, social media has also been used for various types of crimes. In general, criminal offenders use social media with one of the methods, namely: the first method, criminal offenders use social media to convey information to victims, fellow perpetrators, or to the public. When the perpetrator conveys information to the victim, fellow perpetrators, or the public, the criminal perpetrator uses two techniques, namely communicating directly with the victim on social media, or communicating indirectly by only posting information on social media, in a public place that can be seen by the public. victims or the public, or by using social media to relay information to victims, fellow perpetrators or the public.[126] The term 'relay' includes all the methods people use to convey information to others through social media, placing a "like" sign on other users' social media content.

---

[126] Thaddeus Hoffmeister (2014). The Challenges of Preventing and Prosecuting Social Media Crimes. *PACE LAW REVIEW Vol. 35:1*.

In a case in New York, the court ruled that the defendant could be prosecuted for violating a protection order when he sends a 'friend request' to someone who has a protection order against him. According to the judge, the defendant's use of social media to contact the plaintiff was the same form of contact as speaking in person or by telephone and was a violation of the protection order which had prohibited any kind of contact. Thus, giving a 'like' sign and sending a 'friend request' is legally included in the category of social media use.[127]

The second method is the crime of using social media to gather information about the victim and criminals use information collected from social media to commit traditional crimes such as robbery, theft, and other crimes.[128]

OTT Services

Over the top (OTT) services are social media, video and streaming media facilities provided via the internet without a subscription by a cable or satellite network

---

[127] Thaddeus Hoffmeister (2014). *Op cit.*
[128] Tadhg Nagle & Andrew Pope (2013). *Op cit.*

provider. Most OTT providers have their own websites or apps to provide access to their OTT content such as Roku, Fire TV, Android TV, Apple TV, iOS, or Android mobile apps.

The term over-the-top (OTT) refers to applications and services that can be accessed via the internet and are carried out by utilizing network operators that provide internet access services, such as social media, search engines, amateur video sites, etc. The most famous examples of OTT services include Skype, Zoom, Viber, WhatsApp, Chat On, Snapchat, Instagram, Kik, Google Talk, Hike, Line, WeChat, Tango, e-commerce sites (Amazon, Flipkart, etc.), Ola, Facebook messenger, iMessage, online video game and movie services (Netflix, Pandora, etc.).

The speed of development of Internet technology that is used by more and more over-the-top (OTT) service providers and is actively adding and expanding services has become a challenge and a threat for conventional operators who are reluctant to change. According to an EY study (2017), to accelerate their transformation and increase their long-term agility, telecommunication providers must be able to overcome the burden of legacy IT. If they manage to do this, then they will be in a position and can thrive in the OTT world. If they failed, they would definitely have an even tougher struggle. However, many parties are optimistic that the development opportunities in the field of conventional information and communication technology are still promising.

These services are different from value-added services (for example, 'premium call') which were previously provided by telecommunication service providers (TSP). The services were provided through TSP's telecommunications network and value-added service providers are highly dependent on TSP because payment for value-added services was made through payment of bills for the use of services provided by TSP. But now with the development of internet banking, OTT service providers can directly bill their users through the internet banking payment system. This also supports the development of OTT services.

The existing OTT services can be divided into three categories: (i) Message and Voice Services

(Communication services); (ii) Ecosystem Application Services connected with social media, e-commerce; and (iii) Video and Audio Content. This OTT service has an impact on similar ISP revenue, namely video, voice, and messages.

Likewise, non-real time services such as e-payment, e-banking, entertainment applications, digital advertisements, and it is predicted that these services will continue to grow and will become future communication and media services covering all fields such as e-commerce, e-health, e-education, smart grids, and digital economy in general.[129]

OTT Regulation

In some countries, for example Indonesia, regulations regarding OTT do not yet exist, but there is an important thing that must be considered, namely that in drafting a new law or regulation related to telecommunications services including OTT arrangements, lawmakers and

---

[129] TRAI (2015). Consultation Paper No: 2/2015 on Regulatory Framework for Over the top (OTT) Services. New Delhi: Telecom Regulatory Authority of India, p. 8.

regulations cannot simply ignore the effect of applicable international treaties.

Regarding OTT services, there are differences of opinion in various countries in the world, where there are supporters of the necessity of regulations governing OTT, and there are stated that OTT does not need to be regulated by special regulations, it is enough to include it in the scope of existing telecommunications or IT regulations. Excessive OTT regulation will dispatch innovation and easy access to OTT services for customers. Likewise, there are those who argue that OTT application services must be actively encouraged and all obstacles in the expansion and growth of OTT application services must be removed, including barriers from the regulatory aspect.

Net Neutrality Problem

Now the Internet has become a ubiquitous platform, provided for information, entertainment, and communication services. Over the years, the position of ISPs (Internet Service Providers) has been one of the important gatekeepers, placing them in control of the flow of information on the web.

Net Neutrality (NN) is defined as a concept whereby ISPs are obliged to treat all data streams equally, regardless of the applications, services, devices, senders, or receivers involved. They are not permitted to block, impede, or alter data traffic passing through their network. In other words, as a public service provider (common carrier) which is a private institution that provides services to the public in general, they are prohibited from discriminating for the sake of "public convenience and interest." Examples of common service providers include airlines, trains, buses, telecommunications companies, etc. The key word for network neutrality is "non-discrimination."[130]

With the advent of OTT services, applications and providers, a large amount of Internet traffic is no longer fully controlled by ISPs. The increase in internet traffic that is run by this OTT application brings demands for

---

[130] John Maxwell Hobbs (2018). The Battle for Net Neutrality. https://www.ibc.org/trends/the-battle-for-net-neutrality/2633. article.18 January 2018.

network upgrades, but it does not directly return the ISP's income level.[131]

Video Streaming

Currently, video streaming is very popular all over the world. video streaming application is one of the applications with many users and is hosted by various providers.[132] The development of streaming take advantage of the omnipresence of the Internet, which has led many multimedia parties to explore the possibilities for delivering media over the Internet.[133]

The steps that must be taken to be able to provide streaming video content consist of several stages, namely the production, encoding, streaming, and recording stages.

---

[131] Marlies Van der Wee, et al. Evaluation of the Impact of Net Neutrality on the Profitability of Telecom Operators A Game-Theoretic Approach.
https://biblio.ugent.be/publication/ 6868667/file/6868679.
[132] William Garrison (2001). Video streaming into the mainstream. Journal of Audiovisual Media in Medicine, Vol. 24, No. 4, pp. 174–178.
[133] F. Kozamernik (2002). Media Streaming over the Internet - an overview of delivery technologies. *EBU TECHNICAL REVIEW – October 2002.*

Production

To create good streaming video content, people use specialized streaming software and employ streaming design professionals to design the display and sound that will be heard while streaming. For this stage of production, two systems have been developed. The former is called the RTSP streaming platform because it uses the RTSP protocol. While the second is called the Direct WebRTC streaming platform because it uses the WebRTC protocol.[134]

At this stage it is necessary to pay attention to legal matters regarding the content that will be included in the video streaming, namely about the ownership of the content, and whether there is no violation of intellectual rights related to the content.

Encoding

Since the video signal directly from the camera is usually not suitable for Internet broadcasting, it must first be encoded. The way to do this is to use a computer with

---

[134] Iván Santos-González, et. al. Implementation and Analysis of Real-Time Streaming Protocols. Sensors 2017, 17, 846; doi:10.3390/s17040846.

modern CPU processing and live streaming software that can encode the signal and send it directly to a network of streaming servers. In order to stream live in HD or in other qualities in parallel, the encoding software alone may run into a bottleneck, but with the help of a sufficiently powerful computer, one will be able to achieve HD quality and even be able to send two streams simultaneously. But to achieve such good quality with such high performance, one must also use special hardware for encoding, to help the encoding software.[135]

Streaming

The steaming stage is the stage of delivering content to the Internet in real-time to reach end users who enjoy streaming content. For this there is special software to do live broadcasts.[136]

Recording

Once done creating streaming video by using all the previously mentioned features. At the recording stage, special software is also needed to record streaming

---

[135] Sally Thornhill, et. al. (2002). *Video_streaming: a guide to educational development.* Manchester: JISC Click and Go Video Project.
[136] *Op cit.*

content. In this case it is also important to have a good streaming recorder, to be able to record and to post streaming on other platforms in the future including on websites. for that purpose, it need encoder which allows people to record live streams to the hard disk, and also ISO recording, which is recording with the ability to make excellent camera recordings.[137]

Publishing

This stage is the stage to publish the Streaming that has been made to various platforms including social networks. The trick is to forward the file on demand, or by uploading the file directly to a social network, and then take the file and stream and transcode it with the aim of storing it on the server and sending it on request through the server network.

Various video streaming services are currently available in the form of Video on Demand (VoD), including: SVoD (Subscription Video on Demand), which is a type of service where users make a subscription agreement and pay a subscription fee that gives them access to watch unlimited content; In addition, AVOD

---

[137] *Op cit.*

(Advertising Video on Demand) is also available, where users can watch for free, because the cost of broadcasting content is actually charged to advertisers.

Streaming services are now a very big business, for example Netflix in March 2021 reported that Netflix subscribers grew slowly with a growth of 4 million in Q1. In total the company at the end of March had 207.64 million subscribers, compared to 203.66 million three months earlier and 182.86 million in March 2020. Average customer income is increasing 6 percent every year. Netflix stated that the slow growth was not due to competitive pressure, but due to the slow growth of new subscribers.[138]

The legal problem that is quite complicated in video streaming is the regulation related to the supervision of content published in streaming form. Because the device is only an option when creating an account for the service. The creation of a service account is in the form of filling out a form provided by the provider with a standard list of

---

[138] Telecompaper (2021). Netflix subscriber growth slows to 4 mln net additions in Q1, sees better H2. Telecompaper News Wednesday 21 April 2021 | 08:29 CET | News.

questions, so that it is prone to deviations in practice, such as limiting the age of viewers and restrictions on content that can be accessed.

For this reason, the supervisory regulatory system from the broadcasting supervisory authority needs to be improved in order to overcome or reduce the level of deviation in limiting audience/ viewer categorization.

THE INTERNET OF THINGS (IOT)

Introduction to IoT

The Internet of Things was originally known as the Global Standards Initiative on the Internet of Things which was later shortened to or IoT. IoT is an infrastructure that enables the delivery of various services through interconnection between everything, both physical and virtual that is available to all parties, which involves and is implemented based on interoperability between information and communication technologies.[139]

The GSI-IoT activity ended in July 2015 with the establishment of a new Study Group, namely Study Group 20 which focuses on IoT and its applications including smart cities and smart communities.[140]

Internet of things (IoT) is a working relationship between physical devices with the help of the internet,

---

[139] Rec. ITU-T Y.2060 (06/2012).
[140] ITU-T (2021). Internet of Things Global Standards Initiative. *International Telecommunication Union*.

physical devices embedded with sensors, electronics, software, and network connectivity that enable all these elements to collect and exchange data. With IoT technology, a person can communicate with his goods and properties such as houses, cars, refrigerators, air conditioners, vacuum cleaners, water pumps, etc., from wherever he is in the world. It can improve the safety and security of people and their property with a concept called smart home.[141]

In the future the car is set to provide pleasure to the driver as well as the passengers on their journey. Patients can be monitored by their doctor on a continuous basis as they perform their routine tasks. Accidents due to human error can be completely avoided. With the above it can be concluded that the application of IoT will set a new standard for people in their life.[142]

The term Internet of Things was first introduced by Kevin Ashton. He proposed the concept of IoT in 1999,

---

[141] Vincent Ricquebourg, et. al. The Smart Home Concept: our immediate future. Conference Paper · January 2007 DOI: 10. 1109/ICELIE.2006.347206.

[142] M. Tirupathi Reddy. *et. al.* (2017). Applications of IoT: A Study. *International Journal of Trend in Research and Development* (IJTRD).

and he referred to IoT as a connected object that is uniquely identifiable and interoperable with radio frequency identification (RFID) technology. IoT can consist of billions of 'things', which with intelligent communication enable people and things to connect anytime, anywhere, with anything and anyone, using any path/network and service.[143]

With the passage of time and technological developments, the definition of 'Something' has changed, but the main goal of making computers able to manage information without human assistance and intervention has remained unchanged. In 2005, the 'Internet of Things' began to emerge to meet people's expectations, but it is impossible to predict how quickly our environment will be interconnected. The ITU predicted that the number of connected devices will reach 25 billion by 2020.[144]

The scope of the Internet of Things (IoT) is expanding, based on forecasts from various parties that Machine-to-Machine (M2M) interconnection will be able

---

[143] Pan Wang, et. al. (2015). Introduction: Advances in IoT research and applications. *Inf Syst Front (2015) 17:239–241. DOI 10.1007/s10796-015-9549-2.*
[144] ITU-T (2021). *Op cit.*

to peak in 2020, generating huge market opportunities, especially in the machine-to-machine (M2M) and consumer electronics industrial sectors.[145] According to GSMA (2018), there will be revenue opportunities of US$ 1.3 trillion for mobile communication network operators including their vertical segments such as healthcare, automotive, public services, and electronics.[146]

The development of the Internet of Things (IoT), has reached an advanced level and can support and complement the increased capability of using cloud services and with the support of the development of equipment using wireless technologies such as bluetooth, radio frequency identification (RFID), Wi-Fi, and telephone data services. and coupled with more advanced sensor capabilities, IoT has transformed and transformed the use of the Static Internet into the Fully Integrated Internet of the Future.[147]

---

[145] *Ibid.*

[146] GSM Association (2018). https://www.gsma.com/iot/embedded-sim/visited 8 February 2018.

[147] Thamer Al-Rousan. (2017). The Future of the Internet of Things. *Int'l Journal of Computing, Communications & Instrumentation Engg. (IJCCIE) Vol. 4, Issue 1 (2017).*

IoT is the use of internet services for various purposes; from entertainment, social relations and business to education and government purposes. The development of IoT is supported by the development of communication systems, where the 4G system is a derivative of 2G and 3G; Like the evolution between previous generations, 4G takes elements of 3G and makes it better. Instead of maintaining circuit switching and Internet Protocol (IP) packets, 4G moved to IP for all services. The advent of the next generation of 5G adds capabilities and expands IoT services.[148]

Advanced radio technologies such as frequency-division orthogonal multiplexing and multi-input multiple-output antenna arrays are incorporated to make better use of today's spectrum. It is clear that the small changes that have been made to advance the previous generation will not be enough to make the leap to meeting 5G requirements.

The revolution in mobile communication systems continues. Drastic changes to the entire cellular network

---

[148] GSMA (2019). Internet of Things in the 5G Era. Opportunities and Benefits for Enterprises and Consumers.

architecture are being pursued. With the advent of Internet of things (IoT) and realistic UHD services, Mobile service traffic reaches a 1000-fold increase in 2020. This spectacular upgrade requires a drastic increase in cellular network capacity beyond the current 3G/4G network to the next generation of wireless radio standards.

Research on next-generation 5G wireless systems, which aim to solve some unprecedented technical requirements and challenges, has attracted increasing interest from academia and industry in recent years. The need for more capacity is just one of the key drivers for mobile networks to evolve towards 5G.[149]

The Use of IoT

IoT has been and will be used in various human activities, which aim to provide convenience and comfort. Humans never stop to always find a way to get it. Here

---

[149] Michel Matalatala, *et. al* (2017). Performance Evaluation of 5G Millimeter-Wave Cellular Access Networks Using a Capacity-Based Network Deployment Tool. *Research Article, Hindawi Mobile Information Systems Volume 2017, Article ID 3406074. https://doi.org/10.1155/2017/3406074.*

are some examples of the types of use of IoT in everyday life.

Transportation and Vehicles

IoT can play an important role in the integration of communication, control, and information processing across various transports. The application of IoT extends to all aspects of the transportation system (vehicles and road safety).[150] This dynamic interaction between the components of the transportation system enables inter- and intra-vehicle communication, intelligent traffic control, smart parking, electronics, logistics and fleet management, vehicle control, and road safety and assistance. Cars have been equipped with sensors for a long time, starting with a tachymeter, or tire pressure sensors. New ones are added all the time, such as sensors for rain detection, night detection, open doors, etc. There will be much more in the coming years.[151]

---

[150] Hossam Fattah (2019). *5G LTE Narrowband Internet of Things (NB-IoT)* Boca Raton: CRC Press. Taylor & Francis Group.

[151] Constandinos X. Mavromoustakis, George Mastorakis and Jordi Mongay Batalla, Editors (2016). *Internet of Things (IoT) in 5G Mobile Technologies.* (Switzerland: Springer International Publishing), p. 6.

Medical and Health Care

IoT devices can be used to enable remote health monitoring and emergency notification systems. Some hospitals have started implementing smart beds that can detect when they are occupied and when patients are trying to get up. IoT could also allow those people to stay living at home (instead of being at the hospital), but under the monitoring of many IoT sensors, which could monitor various aspects of the person's body, control some actions and remotely inform doctors if needed.[152]

Smart Home

Smart Home is home automation, an extension of housing and building automation, that involves the control and automation of lighting, heating, ventilation, air conditioning (HVAC), and security, as well as household appliances such as washing machines/ dryers, ovens, or refrigerators/freezers. People can use Wi-Fi for remote monitoring by using the Internet. The typical Smart Home architecture divides the communication

---

[152] Constandinos X. Mavromoustakis, George Mastorakis and Jordi Mongay Batalla, Editors (2016). *Opcit.,* p. 7.

network into multiple components: a home network, with distributed sensors throughout the home.[153]

Environmental Monitoring

Environmental monitoring applications from IoT typically use sensors to assist in environmental protection by monitoring atmospheric situations, such as monitoring the movement of wildlife and their habitats. Physical Internet-connected devices used as alert systems can also be used by emergency services to provide more effective assistance.[154]

Infrastructures

Monitoring and controlling management of infrastructure operations such as bridges, railways can be an important IoT application. An infrastructure monitoring system with the use of IoT can be used to detect any events or changes in structural conditions that

---

[153] Constandinos X. Mavromoustakis, George Mastorakis and Jordi Mongay Batalla, Editors (2016). *Opcit.*, p.5.
[154] Waleed Ejaz, *et. al.* (2019). Unmanned Aerial Vehicles Enabled IoT Platform for Disaster Management. *Energies 2019, 12, 2706.*

may compromise safety and therefore improve risk prevention.[155]

Manufactures

IoT enables rapid creation of new products and can optimize real-time production and manufacturing supplies using networked machines, sensors, and common control systems.[156]

Energy Management

The integration of sensing and actuation systems, connected to the internet, is likely to optimize energy consumption. It is hoped that IoT devices will be integrated into all forms of devices that consume energy and can communicate with power plants.[157]

In addition, the use of IoT can also be extended to the fields of agriculture, by developing agricultural machines into smart devices, which can control water pumps and sprayers from anywhere, also in the field of security, so

---

[155] Nina Cvar (2020). The Use of IoT Technology in Smart Cities and Smart Villages: Similarities, Differences, and Future Prospects. *Sensors 2020, 20, 3897.*

[156] James Manyika, et. al (2015). The Internet of Things: Mapping the Value Beyond the Hype. *McKinsey Global Institute. June 2015.*

[157] *Ibid.*

that the fear of thieves can be overcome by using IoT in home security devices operated from anywhere via the cloud. In the field media and entertainment, the application of IoT with data transfer through the cloud from one place to another provides communication between people through the transfer of files from one medium to another.

Legal and Regulatory Issues in IoT

The value of IoT devices remains very important related to the ability to collect, manage, and use data and secure that data from illegal access and attacks which should still be a major concern.[158]

The use of IoT raises many new legal and regulatory issues as well as affects existing legal issues related to the internet. These issues are broad in scope, and the pace of development of IoT technologies often exceeds the adaptability of existing policy, legal, and regulatory structures. IoT cannot be separated from problems in the field of law and regulation. Regulation in the IoT field is

---

[158] Chike Patrick Chike. The Legal Challenges of Internet of Things. *Technical Report. January 2018.*

important mainly because the absence of universal and common standards and protocols can govern IoT connectivity, collaboration, and integration in network structures with diverse forms, ownership and purposes. The use of IoT devices raises the need for new regulations and laws, separate from other forms of Internet-related regulation. For example, regarding the data collected by IoT devices, which can and is likely to be misused and may lead to legal action against users or lawsuits regarding privacy issues against manufacturers of devices using IoT. IoT has also been used in offices, factories, nuclear power plants, and power grids as well as in personal computers, servers, routers, switches, controls, supervisory and data acquisition (SCADA) and creates quite challenging ethical and legal problems, including challenges related to privacy right, security and use of data.[159]

The integration of these smart devices with software applications that power network connectivity, sensors, large-scale analytics, social information sharing platforms

---

[159] Spyros G. Tzafestas. Ethics and Law in the Internet of Things World. Smart Cities 2018, 1, 98–120.

and cloud storage tools has created a new wave of connectivity systems. These internet-connected smart devices, which are designed to enhance and enrich life, have become such a routine part of everyday life that there has been a threat to fundamental security and privacy that has put the existence and use of IoT into question.[160]

In the US, the Federal Trade Commission (FTC) in a Press Release dated January 4, 2017, recognized the rapid growth, benefits, and adoption of IoT applications such as for health and wellness monitors, car connections, home security devices and household appliances, but The FTC also encourages increasing awareness of various IoT privacy and security issues that can reduce user confidence.[161]

As an example of a policy, in New Zealand, the Ministry of Business, Innovation and Employment (MBIE) through Radio Spectrum Management (RSM) has reminded all suppliers of items that meet the "Internet of Things" requirements (lights, water heaters, consumer

---

[160] Chike Patrick Chike (2018). *Op cit*, p. 1.
[161] Federal Trade Commission (FTC) (2017). https://www.ftc.gov/news-events/press-releases/2017/01/ftc-announces-internet-things-challenge-combat-security.

appliances, security systems), electricity, gas and water meters, etc.) to verify that their products comply with New Zealand radiocommunications terms and conditions. Many wirelessly controlled devices are from countries that have different frequency settings than New Zealand.[162] If a product is not compliance with the existing standards and licensing requirements, it will result in non-optimal work and the potential for interference. The supplier must take the necessary steps to ensure that the equipment complies with applicable regulations, by: (i) Ensure that the device has been tested to appropriate standards; (ii) Completing a Supplier Declaration of Conformity, and (iii) Labeling products properly.[163]

Suppliers of wireless devices are also required to apply for a license for Supply Radio Transmitters, to be permitted to supply and import by means of selling, exchanging, leasing, renting radio transmitters, provided the compliance requirements are met.[164]

---

[162] Radio Spectrum Management. https://www.rsm.govt.nz/about/our-legislation.
[163] *Ibid.*
[164] *Ibid.*

In some countries, although IoT is not yet very popular, it cannot be denied that the implementation of IoT will enter the countries in an unpredictable time. Therefore, it is better for the telecommunications authority, as the administrator and/or regulator of the telecommunications sector, to prepare for the presence of IoT.

VI
ARTIFICIAL INTELLIGENCE (AI)

Introduction to Artificial Intelligence

Introduction to Artificial Intelligence (AI) in this book is not intended as an introduction to AI in terms of technology or its manufacture, but only a general introduction to its origin, manufacture, and usage, especially about its impact on various aspects of its use in human life. These include technical problems and various societal challenges and advancement opportunities in life, including in areas such as law, ethics, economics, and the design of systems compatible with human intellectuals.

Artificial Intelligence is not something new, its initial discovery is estimated to be around the 1960s. However, because there is no support for computer technology that can carry out processes at high speeds, AI has been neglected for more than 30 years, only around 2011 and 2012, AI reappeared.[165]

The re-emergence of AI is supported by the presence of super-fast computers and the availability of Big Data coupled with the interconnection of information technology and cloud computing architecture. Interest in the use of AI has grown rapidly in recent years, as it is seen as having the potential to improve people's lives in all areas from medical to transportation and financial services. However, advances in AI technology have also led to growing uncertainty, mistrust, and concern in society as well as in policy makers that AI has enormous potential to disrupt the world's labor market in the years to come.[166]

According to the Financial Stability Board, Artificial Intelligence (AI) is widely referred to as the application of computing tools to handle traditional human tasks that

---

[165] Corrales, Marcelo; Fenwick, Mark; Forgó, Nikolaus. *Eds* (2017). *New Technology, Big Data and the Law. Perspectives in Law, Business and Innovation*. Singapore: Springer.
[166] Henri Arslanian and Fabrice Fischer (2019). *Op cit,* p. 165.

require sophistication.[167] Nilsson (2010) provides a simple definition:

> "AI or artificial intelligence is an activity devoted to making a machine intelligent, and intelligence is that quality that enables an entity to function properly and with foresight in its environment."[168]

While Arslanian and Fischer (2019) stated that AI can be defined as a set of technologies that have adaptive predictive power to well-defined problems and show some level of independent learning and improvement in solving a given problem. These AI applications have long been used to diagnose diseases, translate languages, and control cars, and with the increase in the availability and quantity of data has also resulted in the emergence of various potentials in the use of artificial intelligence applications, so that AI is also increasingly being used in the financial sector.[169]

---

[167] Financial Stability Board. *Artificial intelligence and machine learning in financial services Market developments and financial stability implications.* 1 November 2017, p. 3.

[168] Nils J. Nilsson (2010), *The Quest for Artificial Intelligence: A History of Ideas and Achievements* (Cambridge, UK: Cambridge University Press).

[169] Nils J. Nilsson (2010). *Op cit.*

Beside its positive usage, AI can also be used to commit crimes in many ways. AI can be used as a tool for crime by leveraging its capabilities to facilitate action against real-world targets: predict the behavior of people or institutions to find and exploit vulnerabilities; generate fake content to be used in blackmail or to damage the reputation of the victim; perform actions that human actors cannot or do not want to do due to reasons of danger, physical size, reaction speed and so on. Although the methods are new, the crimes themselves may be of traditional types such as theft, extortion, terror intimidation.[170]

Moreover, AI can also become a target for criminal activity: that is, by undermining the concept of protection that uses AI to prevent crimes or to avoid investigating or prosecuting crimes that have already been committed. This can cause the system to fail or malfunction and can cause damage which will further reduce public confidence in the concept of AI.

---

[170] M. Caldwell, *et. al.* (2020). AI-enabled future crime. *Crime Sci (2020) 9:14.*, p. 5.

AI can also pave the way for evil doers. Fraudulent activity may rely on the victim's trust some AI functions are possible, although not actually used in the fraud.[171] For example, perpetrators use AI as a tool to influence social media users to believe and want to click on phishing links in mass-produced messages. Because each message is created using Machine Learning techniques that are structured based on the profile and past behavior of the user and the content is tailored to everyone, so that it can disguise the intent behind each message displayed. If the potential victim has clicked on the phishing link and entered it into the next web form, then the perpetrator will obtain personal information that can be used to commit theft and fraud in the real world.[172]

Machine Learning

AI is a broad field, while 'Machine Learning' is a sub-category of AI. Machine Learning can be interpreted as a

---

[171] M. Caldwell, *et. al*. (2020). *Op cit.*
[172] Thomas C. King, et.al. (2020). Artificial Intelligence Crime: An Interdisciplinary Analysis of Foreseeable Threats and Solutions. *Science and Engineering Ethics (2020) 26:89–120.*, p. 90.

method of designing a series of actions to solve problems, known as algorithms,[173] which can be optimized automatically through experience and with limited or no human intervention.

In general, machine learning is divided into three subdomains: supervised learning, unsupervised learning (learning without supervision), and reinforcement learning (learning with reinforcement). In short, supervised learning requires training with labeled data that has the desired inputs and outputs. In contrast to supervised learning, unsupervised learning does not require labeled training data and is simply an environment that provides input without the desired target. Reinforced learning allows learning from feedback received through interaction with the external environment.

Supervised algorithmic learning

Supervised learning algorithms require input data to have labeled features. This algorithm learns from the known features of the data to generate an output model

---

[173] An algorithm can be defined as a series of steps to be performed or rules to be followed to solve a mathematical problem. More recently, the term has been adopted to refer to a process that computers generally must follow.

that successfully predicts labels for new incoming and unlabeled data points. Supervised learning occurs when people have labeled data sets consisting of historical values that are good predictors of future events. Use cases include survival analysis and fraud detection, among others. Logistic regression is a type of supervised learning algorithm.[174]

Unsupervised algorithmic learning

The unsupervised learning algorithm accepts unlabeled data and attempts to group observations into categories based on the underlying similarity of the input features. Principal component analysis, clustering, and singular value decomposition are examples of unsupervised machine learning algorithms. Popular use cases include recommendation engines, facial recognition systems, and customer segmentation.[175]

Learning with reinforcement

Reinforced learning (also known as semi-supervised learning) is a behavior-based learning model. It is based

---

[174] Lillian Pierson (2017). *Data Science For Dummies®, 2nd Edition*. (New Jersey: John Wiley & Sons, Inc), p. 53.
[175] Nikolaus Forgó, Stefanie Hänold and Benjamin Schütze (2017). *Op cit.*

on a mechanism like the way humans and animals learn. This model is 'rewarded' based on how it behaves, and then learns to maximize the amount of its rewards by adapting the decisions it makes to get as many rewards as possible. Reinforcement learning is a rising concept in data science. [176]

Based on these three learning paradigms, many theoretical mechanisms and application services have been designed to handle the task of handling data. For example, Google applies machine learning algorithms to irregular pieces of Big Data obtained from the Internet for Google translate, Google Street view, Android voice recognition, and image search engines.[177]

AI and machine learning technologies can be used for big data analysis from increasingly diverse and growing sources. Machine Learning is also seen as an analytical process, including through a deep learning process, all of which are carried out within the scope of Big Data analysis which consists of several levels of processes

---

[176] *Ibid.*

[177] Junfei Qiu, *et. al.* (2016). A survey of machine learning for big data processing. EURASIP Journal on Advances in Signal Processing (2016) 2016:67.

related to human involvement in it. Applications of AI and machine learning are also increasingly being used by economists and others to help understand complex relationships, their use in conjunction with the use of other tools from various fields of expertise.

Autonomous Vehicles (AV)

The legal provisions that apply so far to vehicles are mostly aimed at the driver, as well as being responsible in the event of an accident. With the development of autonomous vehicle technology, the question that arises is regarding legal liability, namely who is responsible for an accident that causes wounded or dead? To what extent do public road traffic laws need to be changed to allow AV use on public roads? And what are the most significant legal challenges in the AV issue addressed to lawmakers, insurance companies, consumers, and finally, car manufacturers. In terms of benefits there are those who say that the biggest benefit of AV is related to the reduction of traffic accidents, in this case AV technology developers estimate that AV can reduce traffic accident victims by up to 90%.[178]

Gradually AV technology reduces vehicle control by the driver, in line with that the law must also be changed both in terms of legislation and in its implementation. Therefore, any research questions related to the legal regulation of autonomous vehicles are increasingly needed, especially in countries that will soon develop the use of AV.

Autonomous Weapons Systems

An investigation conducted by the 2015 Senate Foreign Affairs, Defense and Trade Committee into the potential use of unmanned aerial, maritime and ground platforms by Defense Force Australia resulted in a recommendation stating that Defense Force Australia would acquire an armed unmanned platform if capability requirements were met, and the Australian Government has made a policy statement regarding its use. This policy

---

[178] Adrian Ilka and Viktória Ilková. Legal aspects of autonomous vehicles – an overview (pre-print). Conference Paper. June 2017. https://www.researchgate.net.

statement confirms that armed unmanned platforms will be used in accordance with international law; commit that armed unmanned platforms will only be operated by Australian Defense Force personnel; and incorporate appropriate transparency measures governing the use of armed unmanned platforms.[179]

Public Administration Services

The development of technology, which brings changes in all fields, is a challenge for public administration services which is quite difficult. Since the past, technological developments have caused changes in the use of public services which are often seen as a threat to existing service providers.[180]

Disturbances in the field of public services cannot be avoided, since the past in the field of transportation, for

[179] Senate Foreign Affairs, Defence and Trade References Committee, Use of Unmanned Air, Maritime, and Land Platforms by The Australian Defence Force. (June 2015), https://www.aph.gov.au/ParliamentaryBusiness/Committees/Senate/Foreign_Affairs_Defence_and_Trade/Defence_Unmanned_Platform.
[180] P. K. Agarwal (2018). Public Administration Challenges in the World of AI and Bots. *Public Administration Review, Vol. 78, Iss. 6, pp. 917–921.*

example, there have been disturbances that have led to the abolition of the use of equestrian vehicles with the advent of motorized vehicles. Then the typewriter disappeared with the advent of the computer word processor. The emergence of AI, for some people is something scary. There is a prediction that human labor will be replaced by robots, which are driven by AI and Machine Learning technology. The latest wave of machine learning and AI is unique in it and will affect all types of jobs. AI and machine learning create human-like cognitive abilities in computer hardware and software, and as a result, are likely to have a significant effect on many jobs. In the United States according to some estimates 47 percent of all occupations will be affected. This major change poses a formidable challenge for public administrators and creates an urgent need to act faster than just waiting. [181]

Surveillance

AI technology supports the creation of new monitoring tools to protect and conserve ecosystems, for example to find poachers, and detect illegal logging and

---

[181] P. K. Agarwal (2018). *Op cit.*

mining. AI also enables the creation of software to help locate and automate the world of individual and organizational online messaging systems to support environmental monitoring. At the same time, other AI technologies such as facial recognition cameras, automated internet surveillance and autonomous drones - are ready to be used to increase the ability of states and companies to suppress social movements and voices who disagree with their policies.[182]

Human Oversight over AI

As artificial intelligence (AI) technology advances, algorithmic decision-making (ADM) systems are increasingly being used to support or automate decision-making in almost all public domains, including courts and public administration services. ADM is a coded procedure for problem solving by converting input data into desired outputs and generating recommendations, algorithmic systems are said to contribute to the governance of

---

[182] Peter Dauvergne (2021) The globalization of artificial intelligence: consequences for the politics of environmentalism, Globalizations, 18:2, 285-299.

'algorithms', a distinct form of social order interwoven with autonomous software.[183]

Algorithmic systems are also increasingly contributing to public administration service decisions, whether a person is entitled to social benefits, whether a family will need child protection services, or whether an immigrant is granted refugee or citizenship status. In the future it is hoped that the use of AI in the judiciary can also be carried out.[184]

However, prioritizing autonomy can increase the danger of hidden bias in algorithms for making decisions about who gets a mortgage, who gets a job, who gets parole, and in the changing 'supervision capitalism' of surreptitiously collecting personal data into target advertisement audiences.[185] AI-based decisions must comply with applicable laws and regulations for all areas.

---

[183] Riikka Koulu (2020). Proceduralizing control and discretion: Human oversight in artificial intelligence policy. Maastricht Journal of European and Comparative Law 2020, Vol. 27(6) 720–735.

[184] Riikka Koulu (2020). *Op cit.*

[185] Ben Shneiderman (2021). Human-Centered AI. Issues In Science and Technology. Winter 2021.

It should be noted that AI-based decisions can be discriminatory because they rely on data that may reflect a discriminatory past or look only at correlations rather than causal factors. This AI discriminatory risk can be addressed by leveraging oversight, risk management and controls to meet legal compliance and ethical goals.[186]

Attention to human rights issues has driven the global community to develop an AI ethics, and has produced many ethical guidelines to limit the risks and negative consequences associated with algorithms. Today, human surveillance is supported by various actors as an ethical principle that focuses on the development and implementation of AI.

For example, the EU Commission's Communications in 2019 proposed human surveillance as the first of seven key requirements that AI applications must follow to be considered trustworthy. The risks and challenges that human surveillance is expected to address include harm to human autonomy, lack of transparency and unclear

---

[186] Brad Peterson and Rebecca Eisner (2019). Artificial Intelligence Oversight Risks. Smart board level questions to ask about AI. MLR Holdings LLC. DIRECTORS & BOARDS. SECOND QUARTER 2019.

algorithmic models, issues of privacy and data protection, and discrimination.[187]

AI-Related Laws and Regulations

In March 2018, the Office of the Australian Information Commissioner published the Guidelines for Data Analysis and the Australian Privacy Principles in ethics and human rights implications related to AI. In addition, the Australian Commission on Human Rights also addressed AI in its July 2018 issue of paper on human rights and technology which raised the issue of how Australian law should protect human rights in the development and use of new technologies. The paper was published in early 2019 and final recommendations submitted in late 2019. A website has also been set up to provide information about the project and involving communities through the consultation process.[188]

According to a report from the Global Legal Research Directorate, Law Library of Congress, a regulatory and

---

[187] Riikka Koulu (2020). *Op cit.*

[188] The Law Library of Congress (2019). Regulation of Artificial Intelligence in Selected Jurisdictions. Law Report, East/South Asia and the Pacific, p. 31.

policy landscape concerning artificial intelligence (AI) has emerged in multiple jurisdictions in the European Union (EU) and around the world. The survey by international organizations sheds light on the approach taken by UN agencies and regional organizations to AI. As AI regulation is still in its infancy, guidelines, codes of conduct, and actions by and statements from governments and their agencies on AI are mostly still in the discussion stage.[189]

Meanwhile, surveys in some countries found various legal issues, including data protection and privacy, transparency, human surveillance, administrative oversight, and public services, autonomous (driverless) vehicles, and lethal autonomous weapons systems, it also found that the most sophisticated regulations were in the field of autonomous vehicles, especially in testing of the vehicles.[190]

---

[189] The Law Library of Congress (2019). Europe and Central Asia, p. 63.
[190] The Law Library of Congress (2019). Regulation of Artificial Intelligence in Selected Jurisdictions. Law Report, p. 1.

146

Many countries have set up special commissions to deal with AI issues. However, no jurisdiction has issued a specific ethical or legal framework for AI except in the European Union. In December 2018, experts in Europe released draft AI ethics guidelines that set out a framework for designing trustworthy AI.[191]

South Korea in 2008 enacted a general law on the 'smart robot industry' which, among other things, allowed the government to enact and promulgate provisions on the ethics of smart robots. However, so far it seems that no such provision has been enforced.[192]

Countries that have enacted regulations to allow testing of autonomous vehicles on public roads generally still require the presence of a human driver in the car who can take over the driving function if needed. As an exception, the Netherlands and Lithuania have passed laws permitting the experimental use of driverless vehicles without a human driver in a car on public roads. Spain, Qatar, and the United Arab Emirates allow testing

---

[191] The Law Library of Congress (2019). Europe and Central Asia. *Op cit.*
[192] *Op cit.*

without the presence of a human driver on a case-by-case basis but have not enacted specific laws. New Zealand has no special legal requirements for vehicles to have a driver. However, the government has yet to receive an official request to test autonomous vehicles on public roads. In Singapore and in Ontario, Canada, it is at the discretion of the responsible authority to approve driverless testing.[193]

About lethal autonomous weapons systems (LAWS), countries regularly meet in the Governmental Group of Experts (GGE) which are members of the Convention on Certain Conventional Weapons (CCW) to discuss the application of international humanitarian law norms to LAWS.[194]

Most countries agree that human control is necessary for LAWS. Countries support the adoption of new legally binding treaties to prohibit the use of LAWS; support the adoption of political declarations as a middle ground for developing a common understanding of the challenges posed by LAWS; opposed the adoption of the treaty

---

[193] *Ibid.*

[194] The Law Library of Congress (2019). Europe and Central Asia. *Op cit.,* P.70.

because the basic principles remained unclear; or think that no action is needed at this point.[195]

In April 2021, the European Commission has proposed new regulations on artificial intelligence. The legal framework is expected to help set global standards for AI, while ensuring the EU industry can benefit from new computing developments and protect personal privacy. The regulation takes a phased approach depending on the perceived risk level of the AI application. Application that is extremely risky and that threatens people's safety, livelihoods, and fundamental rights, will be outright banned.[196]

Several AI applications are recognized as high-risk applications and require strict control, including AI applications used in situations such as critical infrastructure and fraud-prone systems such as banking, justice and law enforcement systems, access to employment or education, and immigration. These applications must be equipped with a risk assessment and

---

[195] *Ibid.*
[196] Telecompaper (2021a). EU proposes new AI regulation with ban on risky applications. Telecompaper News Wednesday 21 April 2021 | 08:29 CET | News.

mitigation system, data control and good storage system to ensure traceability, open access to assess compliance with the intended use and ensure human supervision.

For example, biometric ID systems, such as facial recognition cameras that use AI, are considered high risk. It would in principle be prohibited under the proposed regulations, but certain situations may permit its use, such as the search for missing persons, impending terrorist threats or serious crime investigations. These situations require prior authorization by a judge or other independent body and are subject to time constraints, geographic reach, and database searches.[197]

Other AI applications deemed to have limited risk, such as chatbots used for customer service, will only be subject to transparency obligations. So, the user must be notified that they are interacting with the machine before the conversation can continue. Most AI systems fall into the minimal risk category. Applications such as AI-enabled video games are allowed to be used freely, without any special regulations. Industry players are also invited to develop a voluntary code to help regulate low-

---

[197] Telecompaper (2021a). *Op cit.*

risk services and provide guidance on any need for future regulation.[198]

In the case of enforcement of the proposed regulations, the European Commission wishes to leave this to the existing market surveillance authorities operating in EU countries. This will encourage the European Artificial Intelligence Council to support implementation and coordination and help develop new standards for AI.[199]

Further regulations are designed to cover the integration of AI in hardware, from robots to lawn mowers, 3D printers, construction machinery and industrial production lines. Designed to replace the Machinery Instructions, the new Machinery Regulations describe health and safety requirements for equipment. Businesses only need to do one conformity assessment for both regulations.

---

[198] *Ibid.*
[199] *Ibid.*

VII

FINTECH (TECHNOLOGY BASED FINANCIAL)

Development of Technology in Financial Sector

Technological developments currently penetrate all aspects of human life, and have an impact on financial, business, and economic developments. Technological developments have brought drastic changes in the financial sector, namely the development of a technology-based financial system, known as fintech. Things that greatly affect the scope of the financial sector brought about by technological advances include the development of fintech, crypto-assets, and the use of artificial intelligence (AI).

Fintech

The term 'fintech' or technology-based finance is used to describe a variety of innovative business models and emerging technologies that have the potential to reform the financial services industry.[200] The emergence of fintech is inseparable from the urge to get easier access to financial services, because from the past the barriers to accessing traditional financial institutions have been felt by people all over the world, especially the lower class, as Muhammad Yunus said:

> *'Credit institutions decided they could do business only with the rich and pronounced a death sentence on the poor by announcing that they were not creditworthy'.*[201]

This is because: First, traditional financial institutions such as banks and investment managers are constrained by domestic and international regulations that prevent them from serving those in the lower classes. Second, the main business culture of financial institutions is to pursue profit and invest only focused on high-end customers. Third, most business units are governed by Key Performance Indicators that focus on individual performance which is the sole focus of productivity.

---

[200] IOSCO (2017), "Research Report on Financial Technologies (Fintech)," February, p. 4.
[201] Muhammad Yunus (2003). *Banker to the Poor. The Autobiography of Muhamad Yunus, founder of the Grameen Bank.* (London: Aurum Press), p. 255.

These obstacles encourage the presence of fintech that allows information, technology, and capital cooperation to provide a model of sustainable financial institutions that can serve all classes in society.[202]

Although the term Fintech is relatively new, innovation in finance has a long history. It is widely acknowledged that technology has always played a key role in the financial sector, but it is very difficult to characterize the development of Fintech. For example, in a paper entitled "150 years of Fintech", Arner et al. (2016) describe that the development of Fintech has gone through three eras, namely: Fintech 1.0 (1866–1967); Fintech 2.0 (1967–2008); and Fintech 3.0 (2008-present). Arner et al. argues that the emergence of the first transatlantic cable in 1866 allowed the initial combination of finance and technology, culminating in the first period of financial globalization.[203]

---

[202] David Lee and Linda Low (2018). *Inclusive fintech: blockchain, cryptocurrency and ICO*. (New York: World Scientific), p. 260.

[203] Douglas W. Arner, *et. al.* (2016). The evolution of fintech: a new post-crisis paradigm? *Georgetown Journal of International Law (Vol. 47, Issue 4).*

Driven by smartphones and application programming interfaces (API) and further triggered by the global financial crisis (GFC) in 2008, currently Fintech is at stage 3.0 in developed countries and Fintech 3.5 in developing countries. [204]

Innovative Fintech business models usually offer one or more products or services in an automated method using the internet. This [new] emerging fintech pushes for an elegant simplification of the financial narrative. Fintech focuses on the tangible aspects of financial transactions, not with inherently complex systemic dynamics. Fintech is a solution aimed at identified and isolated financial market transactions, and realizing a microfinance system, is not a macro-level view. In contrast to the traditional financial system, fintech is a social revolution in a broader form that aims to rebuild financial markets based on the principles of mutuality,

---

[204] Douglas W. Arner, *et. al.* (2016). *Op cit.* See also: Cynthia Weiyi Cai (2018). Disruption of financial intermediation by FinTech: a review on crowdfunding and blockchain. *Accounting & Finance 58 (2018) 965–992.*

cooperation, and inclusiveness of all members of society.[205]

Fintech is starting to change the way people think about finance. With growing everywhere, the fintech phenomenon is gradually changing people's understanding of the financial system that seems more objective, science-based, and which is another application model of information technology applications and computer analysis.[206]

Technology in finance not only enhances the financial sector but also complements traditional banking and financial services. People who do not have a bank account and who are served by banks can be reached with financial technology that adheres to the principle of LASIC (*low margin, asset light, scalable, innovative and compliance easy*). With the presence of fintech, 62% of people who do not have bank accounts can be served by fintech providers and it has been realized that there are

---

[205] Omarova, S. T. (2019). New tech v. new deal: Fintech as systemic phenomenon. Yale Journal on Regulation, 36(2), 735-794.
[206] *Op cit.*

still many untapped market opportunities with technology supported by Big Data.[207]

The development of fintech, encourages financial service actors to open financial services that are different from the traditional ones previously provided by existing bank service providers, brokers, or investment managers. Examples of these new services include:

Equity crowdfunding platform

ECF is a business model that allows individuals to invest in a company, usually a start-up company or early-stage entrepreneur, through the existing market for that company's stock. Traditionally, these investments were made only by venture capitalists and individuals with wealth that could provide capital for a start-up business, usually entering the convertible debt or equity ownership market.[208] With the development of the ECF has opened a wider avenue for equity investment in private companies for individual investors. Investors earn

---

[207] David Lee and Linda Low (2018), p. 262; Douglas W. Arner, *et. al*. (2016). *Op cit*.

[208] Jonas Löher (2017). The interaction of equity crowdfunding platforms and ventures: an analysis of the preselection process. Venture Capital, 2017 VOL. 19, NOS. 1–2, 51–74.

investment returns through equity crowdfunding from dividends, the sale of the company, or through the sale of shares if the company has been listed on a stock exchange. While this system leverages technology to attract investors, the real novelty is that the size of the companies involved is smaller than that of companies that typically make public offerings of securities to the public.[209]

From a regulatory point of view, the ECF platform can be categorized as securities offering and management, and in some countries, it is often included in the scope of securities regulations.[210]

Peer-to-peer lending platform (P2P)

This platform is a business model that in many ways allow investors, alone or in conjunction with others, to provide financing to borrowers. What is new in this business model is that funds can be obtained from various lenders/investors ranging from individuals to institutional investors. In return for funding their share of financial

---

[209] Jonas Löher (2017). *Op cit.*
[210] IOSCO (2017). *Op cit.*

needs, the lender/investor can earn monthly interest income in addition to payments for the return of capital.[211]

From a regulatory perspective, except for platforms that only provide loan funds, P2P lending platforms often also issue securities or shares in collective investment schemes, and as a result, are often included in the scope of securities regulation.[212]

Robo-Advisor

In addition to the two platforms above, there is also a Robo-Adviser providing automated investment advice and a social trading platform that offers brokerage and investment services.[213] Robo-advisor is a digital platform that provides financial planning services such as investing automatically using algorithms. Robo-advisors work by gathering information from clients about their financial situation as well as their future goals. To do this, the client

---

[211] Yeujun Yoon, et. al. (2019). Factors affecting platform default risk in online peer-to-peer (P2P) lending business: an empirical study using Chinese online P2P platform data. *Electron Commer Res (2019) 19:131–158.*

[212] IOSCO (2017). *Op cit.*

[213] Zhi-Long Dong, Min-Xing Zhu & Feng-Min Xu (2021): Robo-advisor using closed-form solutions for investors' risk preferences, Applied Economics Letters, DOI: 10.1080/13504851.2021.1937495.

is asked to answer a survey or some questions online. Then, the robo-advisor uses the entered data to provide investment advice. This service has the capability to perform analysis with little or no human supervision required. The advantage of using a robo-advisor is that it can eliminate the biased behavior that often occurs with human advisors and can handle routine account maintenance without human involvement.[214]

Other capabilities of robo-advisors include 'automated investment advisors', 'automated investment management' and 'digital advice' platforms. All of this refers to the shift of consumers towards using fintech applications for investment management.[215]

Robo-advisors have the same legal status as human advisors. Robo-advisors must be registered with the U.S. Securities and Exchange Commission (SEC) to do business and are therefore subject to the same securities

[214] Lixuan Zhang, et. al. (2020). Who do you choose? Comparing perceptions of human vs robo-advisor in the context of financial services. Journal of Services Marketing.
[215] Hazik Mohamed and Hassnian Ali (2019). *Blockchain, Fintech, and Islamic Finance. Building the Future in the New Islamic Digital Economy*. (Boston/ Berlin: Walter de Gruyter Inc.), p. 62.

laws and regulations as traditional broker-dealers. Its official name is 'Registered Investment Adviser', or RIA for short. Most robo-advisors are members of the independent regulator Financial Industry Regulatory Authority (FINRA) as well. Investors can use BrokerCheck to research robo-advisors the same way they treat human advisors.[216]

In the United States, assets managed by robotic advisors are not insured by the Federal Deposit Insurance Corporation (FDIC), because they are securities held for investment purposes, not bank deposits. However, this does not mean that clients are not protected, as there are many other avenues in which broker-dealers can insure assets. For example, Wealthfront, the second largest robotic advisor in the United States, is insured by the Securities Investor Protection Corporation (SIPC).[217]

Cryptocurrency, Cryptoassets, and Bitcoin

The ability to potentially benefit from innovations in financial services is highly dependent on the regulatory

---

[216] Hazik Mohamed and Hassnian Ali (2019). *Op cit.*
[217] *Ibid.*

environment in a particular jurisdiction, cryptoassets are the only innovations in finance that have emerged in recent years which are highly controversial and pose a challenge to regulators and policy makers.[218]

The terms cryptoasset and token can have different meanings depending on the context in which they are used. Therefore, regulators in various countries face challenges in understanding the essence of the different terms; to identify the most appropriate terminology that can be used in the formation of the relevant regulations, and to define the terminology clearly and ensure it is used consistently in official situations. Fintech that provides market or economic opportunities, also deal with encryption, password security, or broader digital security.[219]

Digital Currency which is meant here is a medium or medium of exchange that is in a form that is not real (virtual) and not in the form of an existing currency but

---

[218] Apolline Blandin, et. al. (2019). *The Global Cryptoasset Regulatory Landscape Study*. Cambridge: Cambridge Centre for Alternative Finance.

[219] Paolo Sironi (2016). FinTech Innovation. *From Robo-Advisors to Goal Based Investing and Gamification.* Chichester, UK: Wiley.

can be a substitute for currency.[220] One type of virtual currency is cryptocurrency, which is meant here is an internet-based virtual currency in which ownership of a certain unit of value is validated using cryptography. Cryptocurrency is not a legal medium of exchange (currencies) and, therefore, its use for a transaction requires the consent of both parties.[221]

Cryptoasset

Cryptoassets are a subset of the larger category of alternative currencies, which operate outside the scope of regulation and create so-called 'alternative payment systems' that coexist with payment systems recognized by national and/or supranational laws.[222] In relation to regulation, there are some matters that must be

---

[220] Rosario Girasa. Regulation of Cryptocurrencies and Blockchain Technologies. National and International Perspectives. (Cham: Palgrave), p. 11
[221] Sarah Jane Hughes; Stephen T. Middlebrook (2015). Advancing a Framework for Regulating Cryptocurrency Payments Intermediaries. *Yale Journal on Regulation 32, no. 2 (Summer 2015): 495-560*, p. 504.
[222] Gary Marchant, et. al. (2020). International Governance of Cryptoassets: Whether, Why, What and Who? *International Lawyer (Vol. 53, Issue 3)*.

considered, such as the nature and form of cryptoassets, issuance of cryptoassets, and intermediary activities in the life cycle and trading and tax of cryptoassets.[223]

The nature of cryptoassets

Alternative currencies come in many forms. They can be physical (like the seashells that some Pacific countries still use), or digital (like Bitcoin), or both (like the Bristol pound, which had a paper version and a digital version in circulation at the same time). This alternative currency can be in the form of various exchange rates into currency (fiat money)[224] and can be centralized (that is, with a single publishing and administration center), or decentralized (without such a center). Overall, the number of alternative currency options is significant, limited only by human intelligence.[225]

---

[223] Maria Demertzis & Guntram B. Wolff (2018). The economic potential and risks of crypto assets: is a regulatory framework needed? *Policy ContributionIssue No. 14 | September 2018.*

[224] Fiat money is paper currency that cannot be exchanged for gold or silver because there is no longer gold and silver as collateral for the paper money. *See:* Gerard N. Magliocca, A New Approach to Congressional Power: Revisiting the Legal Tender Cases, 95 Geo. L.J. 119 (2006), p. 135.

[225] Gary Marchant, et. al. (2020). *Op cit*

Cryptoassets vary in form and type, but the common features are cryptocurrency ('digital currency'), i.e., Cryptoassets for making payments; Utility tokens, i.e., access applications or services; Asset tokens, i.e., claims on assets or income; and asset-backed tokens, i.e., ownership assets.[226]

Issuance of cryptoasset

Cryptoassets share some of the same features as traditional financial assets, the novelty lies in the distributed nature of the blockchain-based network used, which differs from the investment characteristics, which are naturally present in Central Securities Depositories (CSD).[227] The number of cryptoassets published and traded at the time of this book writing is over 1,800, with a total market capitalization of over US$200 billion. Estimates of circulating cryptoassets (which are available for buying and selling) have grown rapidly in recent years. Since the advent of Bitcoin in 2009, especially since the beginning of 2017, the number of cryptoassets

---

[226] *Ibid.*

[227] CONSOB. Initial Coin Offerings and Crypto-Assets Exchanges. 19 March 2019.

has grown rapidly. Since the creation of the first decentralized cryptocurrency 12 years ago, there are more than 6,500 cryptocurrencies being exchanged, with a global market value of over US$350 billion.[228]

The price of each asset is determined by the market. Cryptoassets are traded on one or more exchanges, and both price and liquidity may vary from one exchange to another. For investors, markets that report the most trading volume provide a good reflection of prices, because that means they are the most active and have the most liquidity.

Intermediary in the cryptoasset lifecycle

Cryptoassets are currently growing and are working to establish themselves as a new asset class. Although Cryptoassets have been the subject of numerous publications, speculation, and price volatility. However, the interesting momentum that is developing includes the use of Initial Coin Offerings (ICOs), namely asset-backed

---

[228] Sheldon Bennett (2020). Blockchain and Cryptoassets: Insights from Practice. *AP Vol. 19 No. 4 — PC vol. 19, no. 4 (2020) pp. 283–302.*

assets and tokens as a potential method of initial financing for small and medium-sized companies.[229]

Cryptoasset security

The current security challenge is the pressing need for regulation to ensure that cryptoassets comply with the principles of KYC (know your customer), AML (anti-money laundering)/ CFT (combating the financing of terrorism) and mandatory sanctions screening. However, the duplication costs are quite significant, and the complexity of the rules indicates that the risk of failure for compliance is still relatively high.[230]

As for why cryptocurrency can be used as money, it is because it can be seen how it conforms to the requirements regarding commodities that are useful for exchange indirectly, namely:

a. *Portability*. Cryptocurrencies excel in portability because they have no physical extension, can be exchanged using any device if people can carry a

---

[229] ISSA (2018). Infrastructure for Crypto-Assets. A Review by Infrastructure Providers. *International Securities Services Association. October 2018*, p. 5.
[230] ISSA (2018). *Op cit.*

'wallet file', and there is no difficulty in sending it around the world.

b. *Durability*. Although these coins can also be 'lost', they will not be obsolete or depreciate.

c. *Can be shared*. Bitcoins can be divided into eight decimal places. In principle, there are no technical limitations to the sharing that the protocol allows.

d. *Security*. As noted earlier, the level of theft and counterfeiting protocols is extremely difficult, although they have no specific means of preventing more traditional types of theft and fraud. [231]

The issues of money laundering/combating the financing of terrorism (AML/CFT) significantly hinder and limit the interoperability of cryptocurrencies with regulated conventional financial systems and have a negative impact on the cryptocurrency market, Therefore,

---

[231] Cameron Harwick (2016). Cryptocurrency and the Problem of Intermediation. *Independent Review, v. 20, n. 4, Spring 2016, pp. 569–588*, p. 573.

many countries make regulations on cryptocurrencies related to money laundering.[232]

To address regulatory issues, authorities first need to clarify the regulatory classification of cryptocurrency (digital currency) related activities and do so using criteria based on economic function rather than the technology used. The boundaries between national regulatory bodies may need to be redrawn to clarify responsibilities. Authorities need to monitor developments closely and address regulatory issues that arise from the global dimension of cryptocurrencies. For policies to remain effective, and particularly if markets develop further and international arbitration intensifies, regulation and enforcement will need to be coordinated and enforced worldwide. But the absence of such coordination need not be an obstacle to effective intervention.[233]

The purpose of regulating cryptocurrencies is largely the same as that of other financial assets and services and

---

[232] Financial Stability Board (FSB). *Crypto-assets regulators directory*. 5 April 2019.
[233] Raphael Auer and Stijn Claessens (2018). Regulating cryptocurrencies: assessing market Reactions. *BIS Quarterly Review September 2018.*

can be classified into three categories: combating the use of funds for illicit activities, protecting consumers and investors from fraud and other abuses; and ensure market and payment system integrity and overall financial stability. Regulatory authorities have several tools at their disposal to address these goals.[234]

Bitcoin

Bitcoin is a type of cryptocurrency or also called a 'coin', which is an asset or item whose existence is not in physical form, but in digital form created by software. Bitcoin has no authority as its issuer. No person, company or entity guarantees it, and there are no terms of service or warranty associated with it. This lack of authority makes people think that bitcoin will be easy to use by criminals and will be a challenge for law enforcement.[235]

If a person owns cryptocurrency, it means that person owns assets that are under his control. These assets have

---

[234] Raphael Auer and Stijn Claessens (2018). *Op cit.*

[235] Robberson, Stephanie J. and McCoy, Mark R. (2018). A Bit Like Cash: Understanding Cash-For-Bitcoin Transactions Through Individual Vendors. Journal of Digital Forensics, Security and Law: Vol. 13: No. 2, Article 5.

value, and can be exchanged for other digital currencies, for dollars, or for other global currencies. Its value is determined by the so-called market where buyers and sellers come together to trade at a mutually agreed price.[236]

Now with the existence of bitcoin, business transactions have become easier, people no longer need to think about the difference in currency exchange rates between countries where they do business or have to contact their bank for payment settlements for business transactions, but simply make payments by simply scanning a code on their cellphone. This convenience is something that is highly expected to support technological developments in various other areas of life.

Bitcoin is seen as the original and most famous cryptocurrency. Bitcoin was created by a person or group of people by the name of Satoshi Nakamoto in 2009 and is intended to be used as a payment method that is free from government oversight, transfer delays or transaction

[236] Anthony Lewis (2018). *The Basics of Bitcoins and Blockchains: An Introduction to Cryptocurrencies and the Technology that Powers Them.* (Coral Gables, FL: Mango Publishing Group), p. 96.

fees. However, bitcoin is not yet widely accepted for all transactions as some consider it too volatile to be a suitable payment method for everyday use.[237]

Bitcoin holdings are recorded on an electronic ledger that is updated (almost) simultaneously on approximately 10,000 independently operated computers worldwide that are connected to each other. This ledger is called the Bitcoin blockchain. This blockchain is managed by software running on computers that communicate with each other to form a network. While there are several compatible software implementations, the most used software is called 'Bitcoin Core' and the source code for this software is published on GitHub (https://github.com/Bitcoin/Bitcoin).[238] This software contains various functionalities that are necessary for the network to exist.

To understand how Bitcoin works, and why Bitcoin works the way it should, it is important to remember its purpose: to create an electronic payment system that

---

[237] Au Vo, Thomas A. Chapman & Yen-Sheng Lee (2021): Examining Bitcoin and Economic Determinants: An Evolutionary Perspective, Journal of Computer Information Systems, DOI: 10.1080/08874417.2020.1865851
[238] Anthony Lewis (2018). *Op cit.*

172

cannot be censored, and to give anyone the opportunity to have the ability to send payments directly from one party to another without through financial institutions.[239]

Therefore, the system must be able to be operated by anyone, without the need to identify themselves or get permission from the manager. When parties need to identify themselves, they lose their privacy and are vulnerable to harassment, coercion, or worse the threat of punishment.[240]

By the appearance of Bitcoin all laws and regulations parameter have no function to the digital currency. Bitcoin is not regulated by a central authority such as a central bank but controlled by the individual users who take part in the system. [241]

Freedom from government regulation recalls the libertarian perspective of the Internet of the past, which held that the new medium of communication (the Internet) created an entirely new 'global village', beyond

---

[239] *Ibid.*

[240] *Ibid.*

[241] Daniela Sonderegger. A Regulatory and Economic Perplexity: Bitcoin Needs Just a Bit of Regulation. *Journal of Law & Policy. [Vol. 47:175 2015].*

the reach of the law of any government. In 1996, in his essay "A Declaration of Independence for Cyberspace", John Perry Barlow stated that governments have no business regulating content on the Internet. He stated: "In our world, all sentiments and expressions of humanity, are part of a whole. seamless, is a global conversation about the 'bit'. Barlow stated: "In the name of the future, I ask you who are in the past to leave us alone without interfering." Barlow's utopian vision is an Internet free from government surveillance.[242]

The world without borders and without government control is expected to be achieved with the presence of Bitcoin, a new digital currency that is decentralized individually to individuals (peer to peer). More than a technological innovation or foresight, Bitcoin is seen as the most fundamental threat to fiat money and monetary policy as a whole: centralized oversight.[243]

---

[242] John Perry Barlow (1996). A Declaration of the Independence of Cyberspace. Electronic Frontier Foundation. https://www.eff.org/ cyberspace-independence.

[243] Rainer Böhme, Nicolas Christin, Benjamin Edelman, and Tyler Moore (2015). Bitcoin: Economics, Technology, and Governance. *Journal of Economic Perspectives - Volume 29, Number 2—Spring 2015—Pages 213–238.*

At the time of the introduction of Bitcoin, there were events that raised more positive attention to the benefits of blockchain technology as an alternative to financial and governmental oversight, namely financial instability in Europe which included the seizure of deposits in the 'bailout' of Cypriot banks; technical problems in big banks that prevent customers from accessing their savings; and the ambiguity of America's controversial central bank program. The rise of Bitcoin was also a direct response to the 2007-2008 global financial crisis. For philosophical, speculative or security reasons, the increasing public interest in Bitcoin occurred during a period of unprecedented volatility in the Cryptocurrency exchange rate, which rose almost tenfold from US$10, then fell by almost half and finally by the end of the year 2013 went up for about US$750.[244]

Bitcoin has fundamentally made distrust of financial institutions a philosophy. Bitcoin is the first decentralized digital currency (meaning it does not have a centralized

---

[244] Campbell-Verduyn, Malcolm (Ed.) (2018): Bitcoin and beyond: Cryptocurrencies, blockchains, and global governance, RIPE Series in Global Political Economy.

regulatory agency). Bitcoin is the main alternative payment system for the global banking system because Bitcoin is a payment system that allows international transactions to be carried out anytime, anywhere with very low fees. Politically, Bitcoin is an attempt to separate money from the regulatory powers of the state.[245]

Another opinion states that Bitcoin is a win for individuals who are looking for a way of payment transactions without barriers and supervision. Bitcoin represents an opportunity for countries that do not have a developed financial sector to send and receive payments without the hassle and high cost of sending.[246]

This reduction in transaction costs can encourage small transactions which will help the development of small businesses and can provide financial access for countries whose financial sector is not yet developed.

Those who doubt it, however, see Bitcoin as a questionable economic scheme packed into a libertarian

---

[245] Zac Zimmer (2017). *Op cit.*

[246] Zac Zimmer (2017). Bitcoin and Potosí Silver: Historical Perspectives on Cryptocurrency. Technology and Culture, Volume 58, Number 2, April 2017, pp. 307-334.

political agenda. They think that Bitcoin users and believers are disconnected from the world's financial problems and do not understand the role of central banks. Worse still, there are many who think that Bitcoin is a haven for criminal activity.[247]

The fact is that Bitcoin has evolved into a powerful disruptive payment system. Governments around the world are threatened by Bitcoin's ideological spin but see the potential of the technology and feel they are in a dilemma. On the one hand, regulation is deemed necessary. On the other hand, Bitcoin resists centralized control and exists exclusively on the Internet, which means that effective regulation can only exist through global cooperation, which is both expensive and very complex. Today, many traders around the world accept Bitcoin as a currency. Furthermore, the US Government has not banned the currency and some in the government have recognized the value of the technology. Despite widespread recognition, Bitcoin is not yet fully understood and will continue to exist under regulatory

---

[247] Paolo Sironi (2016). *Op cit.*

uncertainty some even doubt whether the US government will not ban the circulation of Bitcoin.[248]

Doubts also arise because of fluctuations in the value of the cryptocurrency itself which is considered too vulnerable to issues related to various issues regarding cryptocurrencies. For example, when China acted to shut down cryptocurrency mining, it pushed the value of Bitcoin down by as much as 8%. Authorities in the southwest province of Sichuan closed several bitcoin mines, which account for about 90% of mining capacity in China, where globally, about 65% of bitcoin mining is done in China. The value of the cryptocurrency plunged to $31,760.[249]

Bitcoin and other cryptocurrencies state that they are untraceable, but U.S. authorities. in a short time was able to find $2.3 million of the $4.3 million given to ransom the Colonial Pipeline service to the DarkSide group that extorted 75 Bitcoins recently. This casts doubt on the reputation of cryptocurrencies to hide one's financial

---

[248] Bennett T. McCallum (2015). The Bitcoin Revolution. *Cato Journal*, Vol. 35, No. 2 (Spring/Summer 2015).
[249] OZY Presidential Dairy brief, sources: CNBC, Forbes, and Bloomberg. June 23, 2021.

status and data. While it is unclear how the FBI obtained the private key for the asset, one expert said the 'digital breadcrumbs' on the blockchain ledger could pinpoint the transaction. Subsequently, multinational JBS admits paying $11 million to enable outage disruption by a ransomware attack, the crypto world waits to see if the events at the Colonial Pipeline will repeat itself.[250]

Protocol as Crypto Financial Intermediaries

The existence of financial intermediaries in cryoptocurrencies invites differences of opinion, there are opinions that say that with the existence of cryptocurrencies, financial intermediaries are not needed. However, there are opinions stating that this is not true. Because even though it is not like conventional currency (fiat money) where the financial intermediaries are banking as a financial institution, in crypto currency there

---

[250] OZY Presidential Dairy brief, sources: CNBC, Forbes, and Bloomberg. June 3, 2021.

are still intermediaries, namely crypto currency network protocols.[251]

The bitcoin protocol or other cryptocurrencies have the same depository role as banking. However, in contrast to banks that act as intermediaries for fiat money which can be depository and lending institutions, bitcoin protocols or other cryptocurrencies cannot provide loans. In that case, the ledger will be far from credit risk. The bitcoin protocol also has no assets, so there are no guarantees for future claims.

On the other hand, as risk is the perception of collective value, which in the form of an expectation that in the future the claim submitted is equal to or higher than the current value. So it's a matter of hope and trust, not a problem of guarantees. Cryptocurrency holders must believe that the network protocol will remain in the future, and that claims made will be paid the same or higher value.[252]

---

[251] Scott Keto (2018). Bitcoin is a financial intermediary and that matters. https://medium.com/@ketojo/bitcoin-is-a-financial-intermediary-and-that-matters. Accessed April 16, 2019.
[252] Scott Keto (2018). *Op cit.*

Distributed Ledger Technology (DLT)

Distributed Ledger Technology (DLT) is a term used for systems that operate in environments without a central authority. Blockchain technology is often thought of as a specific subset of a broader DLT that uses a specific data structure consisting of a chain of related data blocks.[253]

There are various definitions of DLT systems in the literatures, and many on the Internet have come up with their own unique definitions. Some definitions are narrow, and some are very broad; and some contradict each other. As a result, it is coherent that a definition for DLT has not yet been agreed upon.[254]

DLT is a new, rapidly evolving approach used to record and share data across multiple data centers acting as ledgers. This technology allows for transactions and data to be recorded, shared, and synchronized over a distributed network of different network participants.

---

[253] Michel Rauchs, *et. al.* (2018). *Distributed Ledger Technology Systems. A Conceptual Framework.* (Cambridge: Cambridge Centre for Alternative Finance), p. 15.
[254] Michel Rauchs, *et. al.* (2018). *Op cit,* p. 17.

Cryptocurrency Wallet

Cryptocurrency wallets consist of a bundle of software or hardware that generates, stores, and manages the private keys of a person's cryptocurrency account. Software wallets, like wallets on mobile systems, also allow users to view transaction history and account balances, generate, sign, and send new transactions to the distribution network.[255]

Cryptocurrency wallets store public keys and private keys that can be used to store and spend cryptocurrency. A wallet can store multiple pairs of public and private keys. Several types of wallets can be used to store different types of cryptocurrencies. It should be noted that the cryptocurrency does not actually exist physically in the wallet.[256]

The important thing to note is the security of the digital currency wallet. Due to the vulnerability of the

---

[255] Daojing He, et. al. (2020). Security Analysis of Cryptocurrency Wallets in Android-based Applications. IEEE Network • November/December 2020.

[256] Rainer Böhme, Nicolas Christin, Benjamin Edelman and Tyler Moore (2015). Bitcoin: Economics, Technology, and Governance. The Journal of Economic Perspectives, Spring 2015, Vol. 29, No. 2 (Spring 2015), pp. 213-238.

wallet and operating environment, and the lack of security awareness of users, account key theft is common. Experts have worked to address this issue, among other things, by setting up a cryptocurrency wallet remote procedure call (RPC) interface. This method finds that attackers can effectively steal privacy information regardless of their permission. Other experts analyzed and pinpointed security threats to the wallet and found that the security vulnerabilities of the Android operating system were caused by the existence of a permission request procedure. For this reason, experts recommend using the two permissions provided by Android to fully control the user interface feedback loop to find out what types of attacks occur and how to prevent them.[257]

Cryptocurrency Mining

Cryptocurrency mining is not an activity that involves using equipment to search the internet to find digital ore that can be mined into Bitcoin. There is no real ore in cryptocurrency mining, it is not by smelting or extracting an ore from cyberspace.

---

[257] *Op cit.*

This activity is called mining because of the miners earn small and limited amounts of new Bitcoins at regular intervals, like mining for gold. Thus, the process is referred to as mining. In fact, Bitcoin mining is the calculation of the value of cryptocurrency assets through a cryptographic process. In this process Bitcoins are mined in the form of blocks which are ledger files that permanently record all recent cryptocurrency transactions.[258]

Mining is not a simple process. It requires investment in the form of manpower, time, and computing. As the time to mine these coins increases, the comprehensive power also increases. Mining requires a huge amount of energy. Energy consumption for mining Bitcoin is estimated at 30TWh which is equivalent to stable energy of 114 megawatts per year. In addition, individual Bitcoin transactions use a sizable amount of power equivalent to

[258] Martin Quest (2018). *Cryptocurrency Master Bundle. The Art of HODLING, The Crypto Mining Mindset, The ICO Approach, Cryptocurrency 101, Blockchain Dynamics*. CreateSpace Independent Publishing Platform.

provide energy to approximately 10 U.S. homes in one day.[259]

Blockchain is a shared digital ledger that keeps a record of all bitcoin transactions. Every cryptocurrency transaction is grouped together into 'blocks' by miners.[260] The party that participates in maintaining the blockchain is called a miner and gets paid in the form of newly created bitcoins and payment of transaction fees. Miners around the world process payments by verifying every valid transaction, adding it to the blockchain and to secure the network.[261]

Processing by miners was paid for newly created bitcoins per block, and miners put those bitcoins into a special transaction block called a 'coinbase' which sends/enters payments in the form of bitcoins to the address specified by the miner. Transactions are then

---

[259] *Op cit.*

[260] Frank Richmond (2018). *The Crypto Crash Course: The Ultimate Cryptocurrency Guide for Beginners! A Thorough Introduction to Cryptocurrency Mining, Investing and Trading, Blockchain, Bitcoin and Digital Coins, and More.* Amazon.com Services LLC.

[261] Sungwook Kim (2016). Group bargaining based bitcoin mining scheme using incentive payment process. *Trans. Emerging Tel. Tech. 2016; 27:1486–1495.*

cryptographically secured before being added to the existing blockchain. Each 'node' or computer connected to the network automatically downloads a copy of the blockchain allowing everyone to track transactions without the need to keep a centralized record.[262]

Blockchain

Blockchain technology is a computing breakthrough without centralized authority in an open network system. From a data management perspective, a blockchain is a distributed database that records a growing list of transaction records by organizing them in a hierarchical block chain. Blockchains use cryptographic and algorithmic methods to record and synchronize data across the network without changing it. Blockchain is used as a technology to generate, store, and distribute Cryptoassets (such as Bitcoin), or it can involve one or more cryptoassets in some fashion, although this is by no means a must.[263]

---

[262] *Op cit.*
[263] Rui Zhang, Rui Xue, and Ling Liu. (2019). Security and Privacy on Blockchain. *ACM Comput. Surv. 52, 3, Article 51 (July 2019).*

Blockchain, which is basis for a democratically distributed and supported transaction ledger, can encourage challenging new opportunities. Blockchain is also used in various fields such as medical data frameworks, energy generation and distribution in micro-networks at the citizen level, block stacks and especially cryptocurrencies that can benefit from the widespread deployment of blockchain-based transactions. Blockchain technology can be a driver of social change and can solve problems which have been doubted by various parties, including in the cryptocurrency field.[264]

Fintech Regulation

Finance is a highly regulated field because this field is the blood flow of the economy and is related to people's savings that need to be protected. Long ago, one of the ways to ensure that people kept their deposits in the bank, even in times of economic hardship, was that banks were tightly regulated and with an acceptable level of risk, and that their deposits were insured, then continuity

---

[264] *Op cit.*

procedures were in place, business undertaken to ensure that a crisis will not spread to the financial system.

But then, the emergence of fintech became a formidable challenge, even though at first it was only viewed with one eye by the regulator. The regulator is aware of the new risks associated with technological innovation in the financial sector which may have unforeseen consequences affecting financial stability, consumer protection, and other areas of interest to the regulator.

The development of technology related to finance known as 'fintech' has recently opened the eyes of regulators and has begun to develop the right concept to regulate the financial sector which is increasingly influenced by technology. Although most fintech players always view regulations as an obstacle and efforts to comply with them require special efforts which are seen as burdensome for technology-based financial actors.[265]

Compliance with regulations and speed of entering the market are two related sides of a coin. That

---

[265] Stefan Loesch (2018). *A Guide to Financial Regulation for Fintech Entrepreneurs*. (UK: John Wiley & Sons, Ltd), p. 3.

compliance is a cost is one thing for sure, and from a larger-scale point of view compliance with regulations means delays. Even before the customer relationship occurs, the company must make sure to comply with all applicable regulations, document it, and then seek authorization or register in the jurisdiction where the company operates.

This process is time consuming, especially if conducted in the wrong way, and more agile competitors can beat companies that view compliance as an obstacle rather than overcoming it with the necessary skills.[266]

However, entering the market quickly without heeding the regulations that must be complied with will have a negative impact on the company's activities and for the company, therefore these two things must be done in a balanced and prudent manner.

However, it should be noted that the challenge for regulators is the fact that financial markets are a closely interconnected system, therefore it is impossible to understand financial services regulations without

---

[266] Stefan Loesch (2018), *Op cit,* p. 4.

understanding the entire scope of financial services and the various products and services they offer.

This is exacerbated by the presence of technology in the financial sector. Emerging technologies such as cognitive computing, machine learning, artificial intelligence, and distributed ledger technologies (DLT), can and have begun to be used to complement Fintech, both new entrants and traditional ones, and bring material potential to transform financial services industry.[267]

The presence of fintech makes the financial scope broad and global, so the regulations that cover it must also be broad and global, and this is a challenge for many parties, including regulators and lawmakers. This is nothing new, since the Basel Committee for Banking Supervision (BCBS; a committee consisting of international regulators) formed the Basel Accords and the International Organization of Securities Commissions (IOSCO) which provides technical guidance and advice in various areas related to securities, and the International Association of Insurance Supervisors (IAIS), which issues the Core Insurance Principles which contain 26

---

[267] *Op cit.*

basic principles on how to run an insurance company, actually the financial services is set globally.

The development of fintech in the field of financial services naturally has an impact on related laws and regulations, and this demands special attention from the authorities and legal experts in the financial sector. As seen from the IOSCO report (2017), regulations for P2P lending and ECF vary across jurisdictions, and may be included in the current securities regulations in some or in other cases.

For example, in Australia there are several authorities related to fintech, namely:[268]

Australian Transaction Reports and Analysis Centre

AUSTRAC regulates any business involved in providing 'certain services' as stipulated in the law on money laundering and terrorism financing (AML/CTF Act), including businesses related to digital currency exchange, where the transaction is organized by Digital Currency Exchange Provider (DCEP). Each DCEP is

---

[268] Financial Stability Board (FSB). *Crypto-assets regulators directory*. 5 April 2019.

obliged to register with AUSTRAC to operate in Australia.

Australian Securities and Investments Commission

ASIC in addition to overseeing transaction activities in the capital market is also obliged to monitor activities related to cryptoassets (including Initial Coin Offerings (ICOs)) which are starting to become a form of investment in Australia.

Reserve Bank of Australia

The RBA also plays a role in mitigating risks in financial transactions that have the potential to have the impact of systemic financial disturbances, and in responding to challenges in the event of disruptions to the financial system. This includes the obligation to monitor non-bank financial intermediation transactions such as Fintech. In this context, the RBA monitors and identifies financial stability risks posed by crypto assets and brings them to the relevant domestic regulators (APRA and ASIC), or where they arise in the payment system. The RBA itself can develop policies in response to the various risks in the transaction.

In Indonesia, there are several institutions/agencies involved in fintech regulation, namely:[269]

BAPPEBTI and the Ministry of Commerce

Although Indonesia has banned Cryptoasset as a means of payment, the Ministry of Trade has recognized Cryptoasset as a tradable commodity and appointed BAPPEBTI to act as regulator and supervisor (Law No. 10/2011 Regarding Commodity Futures Trading, and Ministry Regulation No. 99/2018). Currently, BAPPEBTI is developing an ecosystem for the Cryptoasset transaction market and with the aim of protecting Cryptoasset consumers.

PPATK

Under the Indonesian AML law, PPATK is an institution designated to prevent and eradicate money laundering and terrorist financing, including as a financial intelligence unit (FIU). PPATK's main role as FIU is to receive, analyze, and disseminate research results on financial transactions. In carrying out its role, it has the authority to obtain information from reporting agencies

---

[269] Financial Stability Board (FSB). *Op cit.*

and other parties, both government institutions and the private sector. Prior to the appointment of a Cryptoasset service provider as a reporting party, it is authorized to obtain information from a private sector Cryptoasset service provider on a case-by-case basis.

OJK – Financial Services Authority

In carrying out its duties, OJK monitors fintech innovation and development and their impact on financial stability.

Ministry of Finance

As a fiscal authority, the Ministry of Finance is responsible for managing the state budget through taxation as an instrument. About Cryptoassets, under current legislation Cryptoassets are taxable objects. The Ministry of Finance is currently reviewing the taxation mechanism for Cryptoasset trading activities.

Bank Central of Indonesia

In relation to the use of Cryptoassets in the payment system, Bank Indonesia has prohibited the use of Cryptoassets as currency. Bank Indonesia is tasked with monitoring Cryptoasset transactions in Indonesia, to ensure the effectiveness of regulations regarding this matter. In relation to fintech, Bank Indonesia has issued several regulations, namely: Bank Indonesia Circular No. 18/22/DKSP regarding the Implementation of Digital Financial Services; Bank Indonesia Regulation No. 18/40/PBI/2016 concerning the Implementation of Payment Transaction Processing; and Bank Indonesia Regulation No. 18/17/PBI/2016 concerning Electronic Money.

If it is related to the application of data protection laws related to the use of personal data in relation to fintech, the first thing to understand is that there are no data protection laws that apply globally. While there are generally provisions such as Article 12 of the Universal Declaration of Human Rights and the privacy principles developed by the OECD in the 1980s as a common source for significant data protection regimes, in practice there is considerable variation across the globe.

A fundamental question regarding data protection is whether a particular set of data falls within the scope of a regulation, for example, whether a data set that is considered 'personal data' in Europe is also 'information that is identifiable as personal data' in the United States.

In Australia, a key feature of privacy laws since legislative reform in 2014 has been an increased focus on cross-border transfers involving personal information. The Australian Privacy Act provides an avenue for sending data overseas but requires transfer agencies to ensure that data recipients comply with Australian privacy law principles.

A data set can be privately confidential to individuals, it may also fall into the category of sensitive data for companies. In general, in various jurisdictions, if the data is not related to a particular individual, then the provisions regarding the protection of personal data cannot be applied. Of course, other important legal provisions may apply to impose restrictions that may be used, including confidentiality and confidentiality obligations regarding banks to large corporate and individual customers regarding certain data.

BIBLIOGRAPHY

Books

Antonopoulos, Nick and Gillam, Lee (Eds) (2010). *Cloud Computing. Principles, Systems and Applications*. London: Springer.

Arslanian, Henri and Fischer, Fabrice (2019). *The Future of Finance. The Impact of FinTech, AI, and Crypto on Financial Services*. Cham: Palgrave Macmillan.

Bahga, Arshdeep & Madisetti, Vijay (2019). *Big Data Analytics: A Hands-On Approach*. Ebook - website: www.hands-on-books-series.com.

Blandin, Apolline, et.al. *The Global Cryptoasset Regulatory Landscape Study*. Cambridge: Cambridge Centre for Alternative Finance and Nomura Research Institute.

Campbell-Verduyn, Malcolm (Ed.) (2018). *Bitcoin and beyond: Cryptocurrencies, blockchains, and global governance*. RIPE Series in Global Political Economy.

Castells, Manuel (1998, second edition, 2000). End of Millennium, The Information Age: Economy, Society and Culture, Vol. III. Cambridge, MA; Oxford, UK: Blackwell.

Corrales, Marcelo; Fenwick, Mark; Forgó, Nikolaus. *Eds* (2017). *New Technology, Big Data and the Law. Perspectives in Law, Business and Innovation.* Singapore: Springer.

Dean, Jared (2014). Big data, data mining, and machine learning: value creation for business leaders and practitioners. New Jersey: John Wiley & Sons, Inc.

Fattah, Hossam (2019). *5G LTE Narrowband Internet of Things (NB-IoT).* Boca Raton: CRC Press. Taylor & Francis Group.

Gessler, Nancy and Shrivastava, Alok. Eds. (2015). *Data Science & Big Data Analytics: Discovering, Analyzing, Visualizing and Presenting Data.* Indianapolis: John Wiley & Sons, Inc.

Girasa, Rosario. Regulation of Cryptocurrencies and Blockchain Technologies. National and International Perspectives. Cham: Palgrave.

Goodman, Marc (2015). *Future crimes: everything is connected, everyone is vulnerable and what we can do about it.* New York, Toronto: Doubleday.

Hazik, Mohamed and Hassnian, Ali (2019). *Blockchain, Fintech, and Islamic Finance. Building the Future in the New Islamic Digital Economy.* Boston/Berlin: Walter de Gruyter Inc.

Inmon, W.H. (2005). *Building the Data Warehouse, Fourth Edition.* Indianapolis: Wiley Publishing, Inc.

Kittichaisaree, Kriangsak (2017). *Public International Law of Cyberspace.* Switzerland: Springer International Publishing.

Lee, David and Low, Linda (2018). *Inclusive fintech: blockchain, cryptocurrency and ICO.* New York: World Scientific.

Lewis, Anthony (2018). *The Basics of Bitcoins and Blockchains: An Introduction to Cryptocurrencies and the Technology that Powers Them.* Coral Gables, FL: Mango Publishing Group.

Loesch, Stefan (2018). *A Guide to Financial Regulation for Fintech Entrepreneurs.* UK: John Wiley & Sons, Ltd.

Marr, Bernard (2015). *Big data:Using Smart Big Data, Analytics and Metrics to Make Better Decisions and Improve Performance.* West Sussex: John Wiley & Sons Ltd.

Mavromoustakis, Constandinos X., Mastorakis, George and Batalla, Jordi Mongay, Editors (2016). *Internet of Things (IoT) in 5G Mobile Technologies.* (Switzerland: Springer International Publishing

National Research Council. 2013. *Frontiers in Massive Data Analysis*. Washington, D.C.: The National Academies Press.

Nilsson, Nils J. (2010). *The Quest for Artificial Intelligence: A History of Ideas and Achievements*. Cambridge, UK: Cambridge University Press.

Pethuru, Raj and Anupama C. Raman (2017). *The Internet of Things Enabling Technologies, Platforms, and Use Cases*. Boca Raton, FL: CRC Press.

Pierson, Lillian (2017). *Data Science For Dummies®, 2nd Edition*. New Jersey: John Wiley & Sons, Inc.

Quest, Martin (2018). *Cryptocurrency Master Bundle. The Art of HODLING, The Crypto Mining Mindset, The ICO Approach, Cryptocurrency 101, Blockchain Dynamics*. CreateSpace Independent Publishing Platform.

Rauchs, Michel, *et. al.* (2018). *Distributed Ledger Technology Systems. A Conceptual Framework*. Cambridge: Cambridge Centre for Alternative Finance.

Richmond, Frank (2018). T*he Crypto Crash Course: The Ultimate Cryptocurrency Guide for Beginners! A Thorough Introduction to Cryptocurrency Mining, Investing and Trading, Blockchain, Bitcoin and Digital Coins, and More*. Amazon.com Services LLC.

Rountree, Derrick (2014). *The Basics of Cloud Computing: Understanding the Fundamentals of Cloud Computing in Theory and Practice.* Waltham, MA: Elsevier.

Rustad, Michael L. (2016). *Global Internet Law in A Nutshell®. Third Edition.* St Paul Minn: West Academic Publishing.

Schmitt, Michael N., *Ed.* (2013), *Tallinn Manual on the International Law Applicable to Cyber Warfare.* Cambridge: Cambridge University Press.

Sironi, Paolo (2016). FinTech Innovation. *From Robo-Advisors to Goal Based Investing and Gamification.* Chichester, UK: Wiley.

Synodinou, Tatiana-Eleni, et. al. Editors (2017). *EU Internet Law. Regulation and Enforcement.* Cham, Switzerland: Springer.

Sitompul, Asril (2001). *Hukum Internet. Pengenalan Mengenai Masalah Hukum di Cyberspace.* Bandung: Citra Aditya Bakti.

_____ (2005). *Hukum Telekomunikasi Indonesia.* Bandung: BooksTerrace & Library.

_____ (2014). *Menggugat Moral Bangsa. Studi Tentang Hukum dan Moralitas.* Bandung: BooksTerrace & Library.

Srinivasan, S (2014). *Cloud Computing Basics*. New York: Springer.

Strong, Colin (2015). Humanizing Big Data: Marketing at the Meeting of Data, Social Science and Consumer Insight. London: Kogan Page Limited.

Trovati, Marcello; Hill, Richard; Ashiq Anjum; Shao Ying Zhu; Lu Li, Eds (2015). *Big-Data Analytics and Cloud Computing. Theory, Algorithms and Applications*. Switzerland: Springer International Publishing.

Yunus, Muhamad and Alan Jolis (2003). *Banker to the Poor. The Autobiography of Muhamad Yunus, founder of the Grameen Bank*. London: Aurum Press.

Articles

Agarwal, P. K (2018). Public Administration Challenges in the World of AI and Bots. *Public Administration Review, Vol. 78, Iss. 6, pp. 917–921*.

Alcántara-Pilar, *et. al.* (2013). A cross-cultural analysis of the effect of language on perceived risk online. *Computers in Human Behavior, 29(3), 596–603*.

Alhakbani, Noura *et. al.* An efficient event matching system for semantic smart data in the Internet of Things (IoT) environment. *Future Generation Computer Systems 95 (2019) 163–174*.

Al-Rousan, Thamer. (2017). The Future of the Internet of Things. *Int'l Journal of Computing, Communications & Instrumentation Engg. (IJCCIE) Vol. 4, Issue 1 (2017).*

Andrews, Leighton, et.al (2017). London School of Economic and Political Sciences. *DISCUSSION PAPER No: 85, September 2017.*

Andrews, M. Caldwell, J. T. A., T. Tanay and L. D. Griffin (2020). AI-enabled future crime. *Crime Sci (2020) 9:14.*

Aral, Sinan; Dellarocas, Chrysanthos and Godes, David (2013). Introduction to the Special Issue: Social Media and Business Transformation: A Framework for Research. *Information Systems Research, March 2013, Vol. 24, No. 1, Special Issue on Social Media and Business Transformation (March 2013), pp. 3-13*

Arner, Douglas W.; Barberis, Janos and Buckley, Ross P (2016). The evolution of fintech: a new post-crisis paradigm? *Georgetown Journal of International Law (Vol. 47, Issue 4)*

Australian Government (2018). Guide to Data Analytics and the Australian Privacy Principles. Office of the Australian Information Commissioner. oaic.gov.au.

Bagchi, Kallol K., *et. al*. (2015). Internet use and human values: Analyses of developing and developed countries. *Computers in Human Behavior 50 (2015) 76–90.*

Bagchi, K., Hart, P., & Peterson, M. (2004). IT product adoption and the influence of national culture. *Journal of Global Information Technology Management, 7(4), 29–46.*

Barlow, John Perry (1996). A Declaration of the Independence of Cyberspace. Electronic Frontier Foundation. *https://www.eff.org/cyberspace-independence.*

Bennett, Sheldon (2020). Blockchain and Cryptoassets: Insights from Practice. *AP Vol. 19 No. 4 — PC vol. 19, no. 4 (2020) pp. 283–302.*

Blandin, Apolline, *et. al.* (2019). *The Global Cryptoasset Regulatory Landscape Study.* Cambridge: Cambridge Centre for Alternative Finance.

Böhme, Rainer, Nicolas Christin, Benjamin Edelman and Tyler Moore (2015). Bitcoin: Economics, Technology, and Governance. *The Journal of Economic Perspectives, Spring 2015, Vol. 29, No. 2 (Spring 2015), pp. 213-238.*

Brown, Jonathan B (2020). Casting a Broad Net: The Federal Communication Commission's Preemption of State Broadband Internet Regulation. *Creighton Law Review [Vol. 54. 2020].*

Cai, Cynthia Weiyi (2018). Disruption of financial intermediation by FinTech: a review on crowdfunding and blockchain. *Accounting & Finance 58 (2018) 965–992.*

Cai, Simin, *et.al.* (2019). Data aggregation processes: a survey, a taxonomy, and design guidelines. *Computing (2019) 101:1397–1429.*

Chang, Victor *et. al* (2016). Cloud computing adoption framework: A security framework for business clouds. Future Generation Computer Systems 57 (2016) 24–41.

Chike Patrick Chike (2018). The Legal Challenges of Internet of Things. *Research Gate Technical Report,* January 2018.

Conti, Mauro, et. al. On the Economic Significance of Ransomware Campaigns: A Bitcoin Transactions Perspective.

Correa, Teresa (2016). Digital skills and social media use: how Internet skills are related to different types of Facebook use among 'digital natives.' *Information, Communication & Society, 19:8, 1095-1107.*

Cvar, Nina (2020). The Use of IoT Technology in Smart Cities and Smart Villages: Similarities, Differences, and Future Prospects. *Sensors 2020, 20, 3897.*

Daojing He, et. al. (2020). Security Analysis of Cryptocurrency Wallets in Android-based Applications. *IEEE Network. November/ December 2020.*

Demertzis, Maria & Wolff, Guntram B. (2018). The economic potential and risks of crypto assets: is a regulatory framework needed? *Policy Contribution Issue No. 14 | September 2018.*

Dimitrios Zissis and Dimitrios Lekkas (2012). Addressing cloud computing security issues. Future Generation Computer Systems 28 (2012) 583–592.

Downes, P. K. (2007). An introduction to the Internet. *British Dental Journal Volume 202 No. 5 Mar 10 2007.*

Dong, Zhi-Long, Min-Xing Zhu & Feng-Min Xu (2021): Robo-advisor using closed-form solutions for investors' risk preferences, Applied Economics Letters, DOI: 10.1080/13504851.2021.1937495.

Dumitrescu. E. F. (2018). Cloud Quantum Computing of an Atomic Nucleus. Quant-ph, 11 January 2018.

EBA, EIOPA and ESMA (2016), "European Joint Committee Discussion Paper on the Use of Big Data by Financial Institutions," JC 2016.

Eckstein, James N. and Levy, Jeremy, Eds. (2013). Materials issues for quantum computation. *MRS BULLETIN VOLUME 38 OCTOBER 2013.*

Ejaz, Waleed, *et. al.* (2019). Unmanned Aerial Vehicles Enabled IoT Platform for Disaster Management. *Energies 2019, 12, 2706.*

Fagin, Ronald, et. al. (2016). Declarative Cleaning of Inconsistencies in Information Extraction. *ACM Transactions on Database Systems, Vol. 41, No. 1, Article 6.*

Financial Stability Board (2017). *Artificial intelligence and machine learning in financial services Market developments and financial stability implications.* 1 November 2017.

Gena, Mitsuo and Katai, Osamu (2009). Evolutionary Computation Technology and its Application. *TRANSACTIONS ON ELECTRICAL AND ELECTRONIC ENGINEERING IEEJ Trans 2009; 4: 34–35.*

González, Lennin Hernández (2013). Habeo Facebook ergo sum? Issues around privacy and the right to be forgotten and the freedom of expression on online social networks, *Ent. L.R. 2013, 24(3), 83-87.*

González Iván Santos, et. al. Implementation and Analysis of Real-Time Streaming Protocols. Sensors 2017, 17, 846; doi:10.3390/s17040846.

Harwick, Cameron (2016). Cryptocurrency and the Problem of Intermediation. *Independent Review, v. 20, n. 4, Spring 2016, pp. 569–588.*

Haykin, Simon and Moher, Michael (2007). *Introduction to Analog and Digital Communications. Second Edition.* Hoboken, NJ: John Wiley & Sons, Inc.

Hoffmeister, Thaddeus (2014). The Challenges of Preventing and Prosecuting Social Media Crimes. *PACE LAW REVIEW Vol. 35:1.*

Holsapple, Clyde W, *et. al.* (2018). Business social media analytics: Characterization and conceptual framework. *Decision Support Systems 110 (2018) 32–45*

Islam, Nayeem & Want, Roy (2014). Smartphones: Past, Present, and Future. *Pervasive computing October–december 2014.* Published by the IEEE CS.

Islam, *et al.* Journal of Cloud Computing: Advances, Systems and Applications (2020) 9:9, https://doi.org/10.1186/s13677-020-0155-6.

Kahn, Robert, *et. al.* (1997). The Evolution of the Internet as a Global Information System. The International Information & Library Review, 29:2, 129-151.

Keto, Scott (2018). Bitcoin is a financial intermediary and that matters. https://medium.com/@ketojo/bitcoin-is-a-financial-intermediary-and-that-matters. Accessed April 16, 2019.

Kietzmann, J.H, *et. al.* (2011). Social media? Get serious! Understanding the functional building blocks of social media. *Business Horizons 54 (3) (2011) 241–251.*

Kim, Sungwook (2016). Group bargaining based bitcoin mining scheme using incentive payment process. *Trans. Emerging Tel. Tech. 2016; 27:1486–1495*

King, Nancy J. and Raja, V.T. (2013). What Do They Really Know About Me in the Cloud? A Comparative Law Perspective on Protecting Privacy and Security of Sensitive Consumer Data. *Am. Bus. L.J.* 50.

King, Thomas C., Aggarwal, Nikita, Mariarosaria Taddeo, Luciano Floridi (2020). Artificial Intelligence Crime: An Interdisciplinary Analysis of Foreseeable Threats and Solutions. *Science and Engineering Ethics (2020) 26:89–120.*

Knill, Emanuel (2010). Quantum computing. NATURE |Vol 463|28 January 2010.

Kozamernik, F. (2002) Media Streaming over the Internet - an overview of delivery technologies. *EBU TECHNICAL REVIEW – October 2002.*

Kronke, Christoph (2018). Data regulations in the internet of things. *Frontiers of Law in China, 13(3), 367-379.*

Leiner, B. V., *et al.* (1999). A brief history of the Internet. *Communications of the ACM, 40(2), 102–108.*

LIM, Yee Fen (2003). Law and Regulation in cyberspace. *Proceedings of the 2003 International Conference on Cyberworlds* (CW'03) 0-7695-1922-9/03.

Li, Xianyu, et. al (2014). The Application Analysis of Cloud Computation Technology into Electronic Information System. Applied Mechanics and Materials Vols. 556-562 (2014) pp 5552-5555.

Löher, Jonas (2017). The interaction of equity crowdfunding platforms and ventures: an analysis of the preselection process. Venture Capital, 2017 VOL. 19, NOS. 1–2, 51–74.

Luo, Jun, *et. al.* (2021). Social media-related tensions on business-to-business markets – Evidence from China. *Industrial Marketing Management 93 (2021) 293–306.*

Manyika, James, et. al (2015). The Internet of Things: Mapping the Value Beyond the Hype. *McKinsey Global Institute. June 2015.* p. 7-9.

Marchant, Gary, et. al. (2020). International Governance of Cryptoassets: Whether, Why, What and Who? *International Lawyer (Vol. 53, Issue 3)*

Mcmillan, Sally J & Morrison, Margaret (2006). Coming of age with the internet: A qualitative exploration of how the internet has become an integral part of young people's lives. *New Media & Society 8(1):73–95.*

Magliocca, Gerard N (2006). A New Approach to Congressional Power: Revisiting the Legal Tender Cases, *95 Geo. L.J. 119 (2006)*.

Mastelic, Toni, et. al. (2014). Cloud Computing: Survey on Energy Efficiency. *ACM Computing Surveys, Vol. 47, No. 2, Article 33.*

McCallum, Bennett T. (2015). The Bitcoin Revolution. *Cato Journal, Vol. 35, No. 2 (Spring/Summer 2015).*

Nagle, Tadhg & Pope, Andrew (2013). Understanding Social Media Business Value. A Prerequisite For Social Media Selection, *Journal of Decision Systems, 22:4, 283-297.*

Naone, Erica (2009). Conjuring Clouds. How engineers are making on-demand computing a reality. MIT Technology Review. June 23, 2009.

Niedermeier, Keith E and Wang, Emily (2016). The use of social media among business-to-business sales professionals in China. How social media helps create and solidify *guanxi* relationships between sales professionals and customers. *Journal of Research in Interactive Marketing Vol. 10 No. 1, 2016 pp. 33-49.*

Pires, Ivan Miguel (2015). *From Data Acquisition to Data Fusion: A Comprehensive Review and a Roadmap for the Identification of Activities of Daily Living Using Mobile Devices.* Sensors 2016, 16, 184.

Qiu, Junfei, *et. al*. (2016). A survey of machine learning for big data processing. EURASIP Journal on Advances in Signal Processing (2016) 2016:67.

Ricquebourg, Vincent, et. al. The Smart Home Concept: our immediate future. Conference Paper · January 2007. DOI: 10.1109/ICELIE.2006.347206.

Riddle, Andrew R. and Chung, Soon M. (2015). A Survey on the Security of Hypervisors in Cloud Computing. 2015 IEEE 35th International Conference on Distributed Computing Systems Workshops. *DOI 10.1109/ICDCSW.2015.28*.

Robberson, Stephanie J. and McCoy, Mark R. (2018). A Bit Like Cash: Understanding Cash-For-Bitcoin Transactions Through Individual Vendors. *Journal of Digital Forensics, Security and Law: Vol. 13 : No. 2, Article 5*.

Rosenthal, Arnon, et. al. (2010). Cloud computing: A new business paradigm for biomedical information sharing. Journal of Biomedical Informatics 43 (2010) 342–353.

Rouse, Margaret (2015). *TCP/IP*. Techtarget.com.

Rugger, Giuseppe (2020). The Internet of Things for Smart Environments. *Future Internet 2020, 12, 51*

212

The Big Bang: How the Big Data Explosion Is Changing the World - Microsoft UK Enterprise Insights Blog - Site Home - MSDN Blogs.

Thornhill, Sally, et. al. (2002). *Video_streaming: a guide to educational development.* Manchester: JISC Click and Go Video Project.
TIEN, James M. (2013). BIG DATA: UNLEASHING INFORMATION. *J Syst Sci Syst Eng (Jun 2013) 22(2): 127-151.*

Tsai, Chun-Wei, *et. al.* Big Data Analytics: A Survey. *Journal of Big Data (2015) 2:21.*

Sahu, Sonali Swetapadma and Pandey, Manjusha (2014). Distributed Denial of Service Attacks: A Review. *I.J. Modern Education and Computer Science, 2014, 1, 65-71*

Smith, Daniel. More Money, More Problems: The Bitcoin Virtual Currency And the legal problems that Face It. *JOURNAL OF LAW, TECHNOLOGY & THE INTERNET* [Vol. 3:2]

Shoaib, Muhammad, et. al. (2014). Fusion of Smartphone Motion Sensors for Physical Activity Recognition. *Sensors 2014, 14, 10146-10176; doi:10.3390/s140610146.*
Sonderegger, Daniela (2015). A Regulatory and Economic Perplexity: Bitcoin Needs Just a Bit of Regulation. *Journal of Law & Policy. [Vol. 47:175 2015]*

213

Vayansky, Ike and Kumar, Sathish (2018). Phishing – challenges and solutions, article *in* Computer Fraud & Security - January 2018.

Wang, Pan, et. al. (2015). Introduction: Advances in IoT research and applications. Inf Syst Front (2015) 17:239–241 DOI 10.1007/s10796-015-9549-2.

Ward, Jonathan Stuart and Barker, Adam. Undefined By Data: A Survey of Big Data Definitions. School of Computer Science. University of St Andrews, UK.

White, Ron (2015). *How Computers Work, Tenth Edition*. Indianapolis: QUE.

Wood, Alex J, et. al (2019). Good Gig, Bad Gig: Autonomy and Algorithmic Control in the Global Gig Economy. Work, Employment and Society 2019, Vol. 33(1) 56–75.

Yang, Chaowei; Huang, Qunying; Li, Zhenlong; Liu, Kai & Hu, Fei (2017) Big Data and cloud computing: innovation opportunities and challenges. *International Journal of Digital Earth, 10:1, 13-53.*

Yoon, Yeujun, et. al. (2019). Factors affecting platform default risk in online peer-to-peer (P2P) lending business: an empirical study using Chinese online P2P platform data. *Electron Commer Res (2019) 19:131–158.*

Zamar, Mariana-Daniela González, et. al. (2020). IoT Technology Applications-Based Smart Cities:

Research Analysis. *Electronics 2020, 9, 1246; doi:10.3390/ electronics9081246.*

Zhang Lixuan, et. al. (2020). Who do you choose? Comparing perceptions of human vs robo-advisor in the context of financial services. Journal of Services Marketing.

Zhang, Rui, Rui Xue, and Ling Liu. (2019). Security and Privacy on Blockchain. *ACM Comput. Surv. 52, 3, Article 51 (July 2019).*

Zhang, X., Pablos, P. O., & Xu, Q. (2014). Culture effects on the knowledge sharing in multi-national virtual classes: A mixed method. *Computers in Human Behavior, 31, 491–498.*

Zimmer, Zac (2017). Bitcoin and Potosí Silver: Historical Perspectives on Cryptocurrency. *Technology and Culture, Volume 58, Number 2, April 2017, pp. 307-334.*

Zittrain, Jonathan L. (2006). The Generative Internet. *Harvard Law Review , May, 2006, Vol. 119, No. 7 (May, 2006), pp. 1974-2040.*

Reports

CONSOB. Initial Coin Offerings and Crypto-Assets Exchanges. 19 march 2019.

Datareportal 27 January 2021. Digital 2021. Global Overview Report.

GSMA (2019). Internet of Things in the 5G Era. Opportunities and Benefits for Enterprises and Consumers.

IOSCO (2017), "Research Report on Financial Technologies (Fintech)," February 2017.

ISSA (2018). Infrastructure for Crypto-Assets. A Review by Infrastructure Providers. *International Securities Services Association. October 2018.*

ITU-T (2021). Internet of Things Global Standards Initiative. *International Telecommunication Union.*

The Library of Congress (2019). Regulation of Artificial Intelligence in Selected Jurisdictions. Law Report 2019.

U.S. Federal Trade Commission Report, January (2016,), "Big Data: A tool for Inclusion or Exclusion?" January 2016.

US Federal Trade Commission (FTC) (2017). https://www.ftc.gov/news-events/press-releases/2017/01/ftc-announces-internet-things-challenge-combat-security.

About the Author

Dr. Asril Sitompul, S.H., LL.M is an advocate and senior researcher at the Indonesian Legal Information Center, Bandung, Indonesia. The author worked at PT. Telekomunikasi Indonesia Tbk, Bandung; Lecturer at the Master of Law Program the Galunggung Law College, Tasikmalaya; Lecturer at the Magister Notarial Program Jayabaya University, Jakarta; Lecturer at the Faculty of Law University of Maranatha, Bandung; Lecturer at the Telkom Management Institute (Telkom University) Bandung, Indonesia.